Human Destiny

SIR ROBERT ANDERSON
THEOLOGIAN

ANNOTATED,
LARGE PRINT EDITION

CONTENTS

1. The Question Stated.   5
2. "Eternal Hope."   9
3. "Salvator Mundi"   16
4. "The Restitution Of All Things."   28
5. "The Wider Hope."   37
6. What Is Life?   46
7. "Eternal Life In Christ."   54
8. Annihilation.   67
9. Conditional Immortality.   76
10. The Question Restated.   88
11. The Question Discussed.   97
12. The Question Answered.   106
13. Appendix.   117

CHAPTER I
THE QUESTION STATED.

According to the most careful estimate, the population of the world exceeds one thousand four hundred millions. Not one third of these are Christian even in name; and of this small minority how few there are whose lives give proof that they are travelling heavenward! And what is the destiny of all the rest? Any estimate of their number must be inaccurate and fanciful; and accuracy, if attainable, would be practically useless. As a matter of arithmetic, it is as easy to deal with millions as with tens; but when we come to realise that every unit is a human being, with a little world of joys and sorrows all his own, and an unbounded capacity for happiness or misery, the mind is utterly paralysed by the effort to realise the problem.

And these fourteen hundred millions are but a

single wave of the great tide of human life that breaks, generation after generation, upon the shore of the unknown world.

What future then awaits these untold myriads of millions of mankind? Most of us have been trained in the belief that their portion is an existence of endless, hopeless torment. But few there are, surely, who have carried this belief to middle age unchallenged. Sometimes it is the vastness of the numbers whose fate is involved that startles us into scepticism. Sometimes it is the memory of friends now gone, who lived and died impenitent. As we think of an eternity in which they "shall be tormented day and night for ever and ever," the mind grows weary and the heart grows sick, and we turn to ask ourselves, Is not God infinite in love? Is not the great Atonement infinite in value? Is it credible then that such a future is to be the sequel to a brief and sorely-tempted life of sin? Is it credible that for all eternity—that eternity in which the triumph of the Cross shall be complete, and God shall be all in all—there shall still remain an under-world of seething sin and misery and horror?

We can have no companionship with those who refuse to bring these questions to the test of Scripture. If such a hell be there revealed, faith must assert its supremacy, and all our difficulties, whether intellectual or moral, must be put aside unsolved. But what is, in fact, the voice of Scripture on the subject? The voice of the Church, it is true, has been heard in every age in support of the doctrine of an endless hell; and in some sense the testimony gains in weight from the fact that a minority never has been wanting to protest against the dogma, thus keeping it unceasingly upon the open field of free discussion. This affords sufficient proof, no doubt, that Scripture seems to teach the doctrine here in question. But more than this must by no means be conceded. On such a subject no appeal to authority will avail to silence doubt. The minority may, after all, be right. What men call heresy proves sometimes to be the truth of God.

But how is such an inquiry to be entered on? It needs some scholarship and not a little patient study, and yet it is of interest to thousands who have neither learning nor leisure. Common folk whose opportunities and talents are but few must take advantage of the labours of others more favoured than themselves. And we turn to their writings with the honest wish to find there an escape from the teaching of our childhood. Some, indeed, have used language which betokens pleasure at the thought of endless torment; but apart from the enthusiasm or the bitterness of controversy this would be impossible. Surely there is no one unwilling to be convinced that hell itself shall share at last in the reconciliation God has wrought; or, if the lost of earth are lost for ever, that in the infinite mercy of God their misery shall end with a last great death that shall put a term to their existence.

But here are two alternatives which are wholly inconsistent, two paths which diverge at the very threshold of the inquiry. Of which shall we make choice? If our instincts and prejudices are in the least to guide us, none will hesitate. We refuse to contemplate the annihilation of the lost save as an escape from something still more grievous. But what if Scripture warrants the belief that all the lost shall yet be saved, the banished ones brought home, and God's great prison closed for ever as the crowning triumph of redemption? This is indeed a hope that with eagerness we would struggle to accept.

CHAPTER 2
"ETERNAL HOPE."

There is one volume which cannot be ignored in any inquiry as to the future of the lost. It has made more stir in this controversy than any other publication in recent years, both here and in America; and according to a high authority, it "may fairly be looked on as an epoch-making book, both in the wide circulation it has attained, and the discussion of which it has been the starting-point."[1] Its title, and a glance at its contents, will lead the inquirer to expect from its pages the light he is in search of. No sooner does he enter on the study of it than he finds himself carried away by a rushing, bubbling torrent of impassioned rhetoric, which leaves him at the last with a bewildered, vague impression that heaven is the final goal of all the human race, and that the conception of an endless hell is but a hateful dream.

But though this is undoubtedly the lesson which superficial readers have generally extracted from the book, it is by no means the writer's own conclusion. The following is his scheme:—"There are, in the main" (he tells us), "three classes of men: there are the saints; there are the reprobates; and there is that vast intermediate class lying between yet shading off by infinite gradations from these two extremes." Of the saints he declines to speak. They are "few," he declares, "and mostly poor." He does not suggest the possibility that he himself or those whom he addresses could be of the number, and his description of them would preclude their venturing to claim so high a place. "But" (he proceeds), "if *they* be unassailably secure, eternally happy, what of the other extreme? what of the reprobates?" He indicates the slaves of brutal vice, the most depraved of our criminals, as falling within the category, and then proceeds:

"If you ask me whether I must not believe in endless torments for these reprobates of earth, my answer is, Ay, for these, and for thee, and for me, too, unless we learn with all our hearts to love good, and not evil; but whether God for Christ's sake may not enable us to do this even beyond the grave, if we have failed to do so in this life, I cannot say."

Other statements scattered through the

volume throw further light on this. "I cannot preach the certainty of universalism," he declares. "God has given us no clear and decisive revelation on the final condition of those who have died in sin." "My hope is that the vast majority, at any rate, of the lost, may at length be found." It thus appears that this apostle of "the wider hope," who seemed to us to exhaust the thunders of his rhetoric in denouncing all who believe in an endless hell, himself believes in an endless hell. He thus admits that the conception of "endless torments" is warranted by Scripture, and therefore compatible with infinite love. In a word, the chief difference in this respect between his own position and that of the so-called orthodox, is a mere question either of statistics or of words. Both he and they agree to believe in hell. Both he and they would admit that it is reserved for reprobates. But while they would give the term a wider scope, he would limit it to "a small but desperate minority." Might they not retort upon him that a fuller and truer apprehension of the Gospel would teach him that, if indeed there be hope beyond the grave, Divine love will most surely reach forth to the very class which he has singled out as possible victims of the most hopeless doom. The wretched offspring of depraved and vicious parents, this world has been no better than a hell to them from cradled infancy. If there be after-mercy for the pampered sinners of the synagogue, shall it be denied to these poor outcasts of humanity?

But "the saints" are "few, and mostly poor," and "the reprobates" are "a small and desperate minority." The "vast intermediate class" remains; the class, in fact, to which we all belong. What shall be said of these? There are thousands among us who, we know, cannot be "saints"—for, as the writer tells us, there "is an Adam in them, and there is a Christ"—but whose lives, though marred by blemishes and sins, are still set heavenward. Though deeply conscious that they deserve only judgment, they have learned to believe that Christ died for their sins, and that trusting in Him, their portion shall be life, and not judgment. They believe that God justifies "freely by His grace through the redemption that is in Christ Jesus," and that being thus "justified by His blood," they "shall be saved from wrath through Him." They regard these great doctrines of the Reformation as Divine truths; and, living in the faith of Christ, they hope at death to pass into His presence in blessedness and joy.

If our author shares in this belief he carefully conceals it. He admits, no doubt, that earth's sinners can have no *title* to God's heaven, save through Christ's redemption. But, according to his teaching, *personal fitness* for the scene does not depend on Christ at all, but must be won either by a life of saintship, or, for the vast majority who never could attain to saintship as here defined, and are "incapable of any other redemption," by being purified in "that Gehenna of aeonian fire" beyond the grave. And if we ask whether these are "endless torments," we are answered YES, "unless we learn with all our hearts to love good and not evil." This is our constant prayer and effort, but we know how utterly we fail of it; and in terror we inquire "whether God for Christ's sake may not enable us to do this even beyond the grave, if we have failed to do so in this life." The author's answer is "I cannot say." "I CANNOT SAY!" We are to bury our dead in the sure and certain expectation of "aeonian fire," but with a dim and distant hope that in the "uncovenanted mercy" of God they shall reach heaven at last!

The writer's argument is wrapped in clouds of words, and his statements sometimes seem contradictory, but on close analysis his scheme stands out consistent and clear. The future happiness of the "saints" is assured. They, however, are a minority so insignificant that for our present purpose we may ignore them. The rest of the departed (believers and unbelievers, regenerate and unregenerate alike, for these are distinctions of which the writer takes no account) are cast into Gehenna; but the torments of Gehenna are purgatorial, and sooner or later "the vast majority" will pass to heaven purified in "aeonian fire." And mark, the awful discipline is *aeonian*. Its duration will be measured, not as with us, by days or years, but by *ages*; and in the case of "a desperate minority," "eternal hope" means a hope that will last eternally, only because it will be eternally unsatisfied.

And if any one object that any part of this scheme is opposed to Scripture, he will be told it is in accordance with "the broad unifying principles of Scripture," and that the *letter* of the Scripture kills. That is to say, the effect of Holy Writ upon the minds of common men, who accept its statements in their plain and simple meaning, is absolutely mischievous and destructive[2]. Surely we may well exclaim, Is this what English theology is coming to?

---

1. Dr. Plumptre, *The Spirits in Prison*, p. viii.
2. This is not the only feature of the writer's scheme which savours of Rome. He implicitly bases his statement on 2 Cor. iii. 6; but surely no one who is not too absorbed by the study of "the broad unifying principles of Scripture" to give his attention to a particular passage, can fail to see that the Apostle is there contrasting, not the letter of Scripture with the spirit of it, but the old covenant with the new, law with grace.

    The texts to which the writer refers in support of his position shall be considered in the sequel. It is enough to say here that most of them have no special bearing on the question in dispute (see App. I. *post*), and the rest are of no account for the author's purpose, unless they be construed to teach the universalism which he himself repudiates. As for his remarks on the word αἰώνιος, nothing further need be said than he himself has elsewhere said in answer to his critics: "Some of the greatest masters of Greek, both in classical times and among the fathers, saw quite clearly that though the word might connote endlessness, by being attributively added to endless things, it had in itself no such meaning."

CHAPTER 3
"SALVATOR MUNDI"

The author referred to in the preceding chapter has publicly acknowledged that while preparing the sermons which form the basis of his book, he was "largely indebted" to an earlier work on this same subject. The volume alluded to is from the pen of a noted expositor of Scripture, and it has obtained such a wide circulation, and is held in such high authority in the controversy, that it is impossible to pass it by unnoticed.

"The Question Raised" is the title of the opening chapter. If, the writer asks, Tyre and Sidon and the cities of the plain would have repented had they seen the mighty works of Christ, are they never to see Him? Are they to be damned for not having seen Him? Must there not be a "place of repentance" for such in the under-world? Suffice it here to say that this question is altogether wide of the real issue in this controversy, which is not whether the destiny of all mankind is fixed at death, but whether all mankind shall yet be saved, including those who have rejected the full revelation of the Gospel.

The author then proceeds to fix the "limits of the argument." The appeal is to the Bible; but before he will open the Bible he must insist that reason and conscience are also to have a voice. That is to say, the question is what the lawgiver has decreed against the criminal, and the criminal himself is practically to formulate the answer. The next point is that the Old Testament, the Book of Revelation, and the parables of our Lord, are all to be eliminated from the inquiry. No one has a right to insist on such conditions, but yet they might be accepted without endangering the issue, provided always, first, that it is only the symbolic visions of the Apocalypse which are to be excluded and, secondly, that the Scriptures themselves, and not the critic, shall decide what is "parable" and what is not.[1]

Next comes the inevitable protest against the use of the words "damnation," "hell," and "everlasting." Much of what is said about the first of these words is true, and would be helpful if written in any other connection. As for the second, he argues that whereas *Hades and Gehenna* both refer to the intermediate state, "our 'hell' denotes the final and everlasting torment of the wicked," and therefore it should be banished from our language altogether. The fact is, that so far from this being the only meaning of "hell," it is a meaning which the word scarcely possesses at all in classical English. It is only they who believe that Gehenna indicates the final state who have any right to object that "hell" is a mistranslation.

A word about this Gehenna. The writer tells us how the beautiful valley of Hinnom, under the south-western wall of Jerusalem, in time "became the common cesspool of the city, into which offal was cast, and the carcases of animals, and even the bodies of great criminals who had lived a life so vile as to be judged unworthy of decent burial. Worms preyed on their corrupting flesh, and fires were kept burning lest the pestilential infection should rise from the valley and float through the streets of Jerusalem." Such is the author's own description. And what is the moral he would draw from it? That the offal and the carcases were thrown there to purify and fit them for some high and noble use! It is amazing how any one can be so blind as not to see in this a figure the most graphic and terrible of utter and hopeless destruction.

Two more chapters being thus accounted for, in the fifth and sixth the author takes up the words which are variously rendered in our English Bible to express infinite duration. "If (he pleads) these words really carried *in themselves* the sense of eternity or everlastingness, they could not possibly have been applied," as, in fact, they were applied, to what was material or transitory. Will the author specify any words which carry *in themselves* this meaning, or indeed any meaning whatsoever?

What is true of most words is true in a special degree of these; chameleon-like, they take a colour from what they touch, and their significance must in every case be settled by the subject-matter and the context. "Words are the counters of wise men, the money of fools :" these teachers one and all seem to take them for more than counters. Every tyro in philology is aware that it is the use of a word which decides its meaning; and to be guided only by its derivation is as unwise as it would be to accept a man of sixty on a character given to him when a schoolboy. But yes, the author tells us there is a word "which unquestionably means 'for ever.'" This word, however, occurs only twice in the New Testament, and in one of these two passages, as he himself notices, it unquestionably does not mean "for ever."[2]

But the author's disquisition upon the "Greek word *aiōn* and its derivative, must by no means be dismissed thus lightly. With other writers such a discussion is mere skirmishing; here it is vital to his scheme. These words, he declares, "so far from denoting either that which is above time, or that which will outlast time, are saturated through and through with the thought and element of time."

19

This needs looking into. The heathen philosophers and poets had probably no thought of "Eternity" as distinguished from time.[3] Their conception was limited to the aeon which includes all time, but that these words were used to express that conception is admitted. It is further admitted that the New Testament unfolds an "economy of times and seasons," many "ages" heading up in one great "age" within which all the manifold purposes of God in relation to earth shall be fulfilled. Here again these same words are applicable and are used.

But revelation has taught men a higher conception of eternity than the heathen ever grasped. How then could such a conception be expressed in the language of ancient Greece, a language formed upon and moulded by the thoughts of a heathen nation? To invent a word is impossible, and yet words are but counters. Therefore when translating the sacred Hebrew into Greek the Rabbis could only take up some of the counters ready to their hand, and, as it were, restamp them to mark a higher value than they had formerly possessed. Thus, when they came on statements such as that of the 90th Psalm, "From everlasting to everlasting, thou art God," they could but fall back on this very word *aiōn*.[4]

Now the New Testament is written in the language of the Septuagint version of the Old; not in the language of heathen Greece, but in that language as moulded and elevated by contact with the God-breathed Scriptures. Many a word had thus gained a fuller or a higher meaning than ordinarily pertained to it. The question here, therefore, is not what is the meaning of *aiōn* and *aiōnios* in the classics, but what was the thought of the inspired writers in such passages as that above quoted. The "aeonian" scholarship of Christendom has recognised that they are used to express eternity in the fullest sense, and this conclusion is wholly unaffected by our author's bold denial of it.

But let us for the moment accept the author's theory, and see what it will lead to. Brushing aside all other considerations, let us come at once to the foundations of our faith, and see how they will bear this new "doctrine of the aeons." If it be true, the sacrifice of Calvary is no longer what we dreamed it was, the climax of a Divine purpose formed in a bygone eternity when the Word was alone with God, and the supreme and final display for all eternity to come of God's great love to man. The author will tell us that "the historical cross of Christ was but a manifestation within the bounds of time and space of the eternal passion of the Father"—a passion which "must continue to manifest itself in appropriate forms through all the ages and changes of time." And lest charity should put an innocent interpretation on this language, and thus destroy his argument, he repeats his thought in still plainer words: "If God has once shown that

He will make any sacrifice for the salvation of the guilty, must not that be always true of Him? Must He not continue to manifest His blended severity and mercy in the ages to come?"

As we hear the Cross of Christ thus lowered and degraded, we cannot but demand, What part then can it have in man's redemption? and as far as the author can enlighten us the answer must be, practically *none*. He shall speak for himself. Here is his new Gospel of "the larger hope."

"The Scriptures, then, have much to teach us of the future, though not much of the final, estate of men. And what they teach, in so far at least as we have been able to gather it up, comes to this. No man is wholly good, no man wholly bad. *Still some men may fairly be called good on the whole*, although much sin and imperfection still cleaves to them; *others may fairly be called bad on the whole*, although there is still much in them that is good, and still more which is capable of becoming good. When we die, we shall all receive the due recompense of our deeds, of all our deeds, whether they have been good or whether they have been bad. *If* by the grace of God *we have been good on the whole*, we may hope to rise into a large and happy spiritual kingdom, in which all that is pure and noble and kind in us will develop into new vigour and clothe itself with new beauty; in which also we shall find the very discipline we need in order that we may be wholly purged from sin and imperfection; in which we may undo much that we have done wrongly, do again and with perfect grace that which we have done imperfectly, become what we have wished and aimed to be, achieve what we have longed to achieve, attain the wisdom, the gifts and powers and graces to which we have aspired; in which, above all, we may be engaged in errands of usefulness and compassion, by which the purpose of the Divine love and grace will be fully accomplished. *If we have been bad on the whole* we may hope—and we ought to hope for it—to pass into a painful discipline so keen and searching that we shall become conscious of our sins and feel that we are only receiving the due reward of them; but since there has been some good in us, and this good is capable of being drawn out and disentangled from the evil which clouded and marred it, we may also hope, by the very discipline and torment of our spirits, to be led to repentance, and, through repentance, unto life; we may hope that the disclosures of the spiritual world will take a spiritual effect upon us, gradually raising and renewing us till we too are prepared to enter the Paradise of God and behold the presence of the Lord and the glory of His power: we may hope that our friends who have already been redeemed will pity us and minister to us, bringing us not simply a cup of cold water to cool our tongue, but words of instruction and life. And as for the great mass of our fellow-men, we may hope and believe that those who have had no chance of salvation here will have one there; that those who have had *a poor chance* will get a better one; that those who have had *a good chance* and lost it will get a new but a severer chance, and even as they suffer the inevitable results of their folly and sin will feel 'the hands that reach through darkness, moulding men.'

"This, *on the whole,* I take to be the teaching of Scripture concerning the lot of men in the age to come,—a teaching which enables us to see 'beneath the abyss of hell a bottomless abyss of love.' And if it clash with some dogmas that we have held and some interpretations which are familiar to us, it nevertheless accords, not with 'the mind of Christ' only, but also with the dictates of Reason and Conscience, the voices of God within the soul. It presents no such sudden break in our life as, in the teeth of all probability, we have been wont to conceive; no heaven for which we feel that even t*he best of us must be unfi*t, no hell which is *a monstrous offence to our sense of justice.* It promises to every man *the mercy of justice,* of a due reward for all he has been and done; and, while it impresses on us the utter hatefulness and misery of sin, it holds out to every one of us the prospect of being redeemed from all sin and uncleanness by that just God Who is also a Saviour. Nor does it less accord with *the demands of Science* than with the dictates of Reason and the Moral Sense; for it carries on the evolution of the human race through all the ages to come. And, therefore, let others think as they will, and cherish what trust they will: but as for us, with the Apostle of the Gentiles, our own Apostle, 'we trust in the living God Who is the Saviour of all men.'"[5]

This is not an isolated paragraph snatched from its context; it is the author's recapitulation, the closing passage of his book. We read it again and again, and study it with bewildered wonder. The question here is no longer of the doom of the lost, but of the truth of Christianity. Of the vital and characteristic truths of our religion there is not so much as *one* which it does not ignore or deny. The righteousness of God, the grace of God, man's ruin, redemption through the blood of Christ, the forgiveness of sins, the justification of the believer by grace through redemption, eternal life as the free gift of God, the resurrection of the just in the image of the heavenly, and of the unjust to appear at the last great judgment—not a trace of one of these foundation doctrines of our faith remains. And what is offered us instead? The weakness of an easy-going deity who will strike an average between good and evil, sending those who are "good on the whole" to a purgatorial paradise, and those who are "bad on the whole" to a purgatorial hell. A redemption "to be achieved in due time" for men with the aid of "the aeonial fire, which alone could burn out their sins," and "the aeonial Spirit," who "will still be at work for the regeneration of the race." Instead of eternal life, we have "the spiritual life distinctive of the Christian aeons"; and eternal punishment is but "the punishment which those *inflict on themselves* who adjudge themselves unworthy of that life."[6]

"This, on the whole," he takes to be "the teaching of Scripture concerning the lot of men in the age to come." "The teaching of Scripture!" It was not thus the Church's million martyrs read the mingled warnings and promises of God. Such views are utterly opposed to the great creeds of the Reformation and the older creeds of Christendom. The author's scheme renders due homage doubtless to that miserable bantling of modern science, evolution; but whether it accords with "the dictates of reason" we are not concerned to discuss. It is enough to be assured that it is not Christianity[7] — it is not even a bastard Judaism; it is the most utter heathenism, concealed by the thinnest possible veneer of Christian phraseology.

---

1. He has no warrant for including in the category the closing passage of Matt. xxv. and the latter half of Luke xvi.
2. ἀΐδιος. Rom. ,i. 20, and Jude vi., where the "everlasting chains" are only "until the day of judgment."
3. I do not stop to inquire whether such a conception be possible apart from revelation. The inquiry would be most appropriate if my subject were the Kantian philosophy and not the destiny of mankind.
4. Psalm lxxxix. (xc.) 2, (lxx), the Hebrew being *Meolám adolám.*

5. Throughout the quotation the italics are my own. I have reluctantly quoted at such length that the reader may be enabled to judge what this doctrine implies. To refute the errors, expressed and implied, of this book, would involve a treatise upon each one of the fundamental truths of Christianity. If any can read the above extract unshocked by the heathen darkness and contemptuous unbelief which characterise it, it is idle to discuss the matter with them within the limits of the present volume. If any one thinks this language too strong, let him turn back upon the quotation and seek to find where there is room for redemption in the writer's scheme. It is a deliberate and systematic denial of Christianity.
6. The words in inverted commas in the above paragraph are quoted from other parts of the book.
7. Finding, perhaps, that even in this infidel age the unchristianity of his book was too pronounced, the author has published "a sequel," in which he attempts to restate the question "as a part of the Christian doctrine of atonement." But the "sequel" restates with increased definiteness his dogma of retribution, which denies "the Christian doctrine of atonement" altogether. It then offers as "a new argument" for his views, the theory that there is a "surface current" and a "deeper current" in Scripture, the former of which is false, as Israel's hope of the promised messianic kingdom! Next comes a disquisition on i Cor. v. 5 (as proving that "destruction may be a condition of salvation"), and on demoniacal possession in connection therewith. As the result, the veneer is somewhat strengthened perhaps, but the heathenism remains.

CHAPTER 4
"THE RESTITUTION OF ALL THINGS."

Every step in this inquiry is discouraging. But a good cause may suffer from injudicious advocacy, and it must not he assumed that the "wider hope" is false, because its latest champions have thus discredited it. With a sense of relief we turn to another book, which both these writers have singled out for special commendation. Here at last we find ourselves in the calm atmosphere of reverent and patient study of the Scriptures, to the sacredness and authority of which the author gives a noble testimony. The volume might with fairness be adopted as a handbook in the controversy; but it may be better, while giving it the attention it so well deserves, to pass on to a discussion of the subject on a wider basis. The writer has the courage of his convictions.

Taking his stand upon the great sacrifice of Calvary, he proclaims the gospel of universal restoration. Not only fallen men, but fallen angels, shall share in it. Not even Satan shall be excluded. This is truly a glorious anticipation : this is indeed to "think noble things of God." Who is there who would not crave to find a warrant for accepting it as true?

Certain points in the writer's argument are peculiar, and claim special notice. "The letter of Scripture" (he declares) "is a veil quite as much as a revelation, hiding while it reveals, and yet revealing while it hides; presenting to the eye something very different from that which is within." This naturally prepares the reader to find meanings he never thought of assigned to various passages of Scripture. And as a signal instance of this, to which continued emphasis is given throughout the volume, the author points to the law of the firstborn and the law of the firstfruits as affording "the key to one part of the apparent contradiction between mercy 'upon all' and yet 'the election' of a "little flock.'" The firstborn and the firstfruits are the 'few' and 'little flock'; but these, though first delivered from the curse, have a relation to the whole creation, which shall be saved in the appointed times by the first-born seed, that is by Christ and His body, through those appointed baptisms, whether of fire or water, which are required to bring about 'the restitution of all things.'" Passing by the extraordinary theory stated here and elsewhere in the book, that creation will be saved in part by the Church, this appeal to the types needs looking into

It is admitted that the firstfruits included the harvest of *which it was a part*, and the redemption of the firstborn secured that of the families *to which they belonged*. If then it can be proved from Scripture that the harvest of the saved shall include the whole Adamic race, and that "the elect" are "kinsmen" to them, this type will serve to *illustrate* the truth. But the first-fruits had no relation save to the harvest of the favoured land, and the redemption of the firstborn was side by side with judgment on the Egyptians, the tribes of the wilderness and the nations of Canaan. Therefore while these types are a real difficulty in the way of those who would limit redemption to "the Church of the firstborn," they seem no less inconsistent with the author's own position. If types can be thus used at all, they establish the views of those who hold a place between these two extremes. The sheaf of the firstfruits, the wave-loaves of Pentecost, and the great festival of harvest will have their dispensational fulfilment in the ever-widening circle of blessing upon earth; but if the final harvest will include the lost of *previous* dispensations, this must be established from other scriptures, for there is nothing in the type to correspond with it.

But further: our author here avers that the whole creation shall be saved through the appointed baptisms, whether of fire or water. So elsewhere he says the fearful and unbelieving must reach the new creation through the lake of fire. This is no flourish of rhetoric, but the sober statement of a doctrine repeated again and again throughout the book, and vital to the writer's argument, that death is the only way to life, judgment the only means of deliverance, Not, be it observed, the death of the Sin-bearer, the judgment which *He* bore; but death and judgment absolutely. Death and judgment lead to life and deliverance, so that the sinner's doom becomes a pledge and means of his ultimate salvation. And this he assumes as an axiom of theology! Let us notwithstanding, refusing to be prejudiced against a cause which seems to need such arguments, turn with open mind to pursue the inquiry.

No candid person will dispute that the revelation of Divine love creates a presumption against the possibility of eternal punishment. On the other hand, it is still more dishonest to deny—and in fact it is admitted—that certain passages of Scripture support the doctrine. The fairest mode, therefore, in which this inquiry can possibly be entered on is to dismiss for the moment both the presumption against, and the texts in favour of, the "orthodox" belief, and to consider without any bias the passages which are used to prove universal reconciliation. If these should be found to teach that doctrine unequivocally, the question is at an end, for in a seeming conflict of texts the presumption against endless misery must turn the scale. But more than this: even should these Scriptures seem of doubtful meaning, we shall be prepared to lean towards the broader interpretation, provided only that such a rendering will neither disturb foundation truths, nor land us in difficulties akin to those we seek escape from.

We may at once dismiss from notice three classes of texts which are much in vogue with writers on this question. The first consists of passages which testify to the boundlessness of Divine mercy and love. It is impossible to estimate too highly the love and grace of God; but it is the merest trifling to suppose that creatures like ourselves, with minds so limited in capacity, and moreover so warped by sin, can decide what measure of punishment is inconsistent with infinite love.[1] Then again, we must entirely ignore the numberless predictions of a reign of righteousness and peace on earth in days to come. These, though freely used in this controversy, have no bearing on it whatever, unless indeed it be to indicate that at the last great harvest-home, the proportion of the blessed to the lost of earth may prove, perchance, to be vastly greater than a narrow theology supposes.² And this suggests the third class of texts above referred to—namely, those which speak in general terms of the triumphs of redemption. A noted example will be found in the great Eden promise that the Seed of the woman should bruise the serpent's head. Does the truth of this rest on the statistics of the Judgment Day? In Christ's triumph over Satan does victory depend, as in some of the games of our childhood, upon which side has the larger following? The suspicion is irresistible that they who argue thus have but a poor appreciation of the moral glories of redemption.

It will be found, however, that the special texts which are the very foundation of universalism really come within neither of these categories. But, it will be asked, does not Scripture speak of the restitution of all? The answer is emphatically No. The passage which is thus perverted speaks of "the times of the restitution of all things," of which every prophet testified, from Moses to Malachi.³ Was the burden of their prophecies the final state? The answer shall be given by one of the authors already quoted: "It is as certainly true as any such wide proposition can be, that the psalmists and prophets of old time never got more than momentary and partial glimpses of the life to come." Therefore, he argues, the Old Testament "will be of no avail to us" in considering this question; and yet he cites and relies upon a quotation from the New Testament which is expressly declared to refer to the very prophecies that foretell a reign of righteousness and peace *on earth.*

But does not St. Paul speak of the reconciliation of all things? Assuredly he does: not, however, as a hope to be realised in eternity to come, but as a present truth—a fact accomplished in the death of Christ. In keeping with this, and as a part of it, God has revealed Himself as the Saviour of all men; Christ has been manifested as "a ransom for all," the propitiation for "the whole world." But will these teachers tell us how men can be reconciled who refuse the reconciliation; how sinners can be saved who reject the Saviour; how the lost can be restored who trample under foot the propitiation? It is these very truths which make the sinner's doom irreversible and hopeless.

It would be unpardonable to attempt to write upon this question without having formed a deliberate judgment upon every text of Scripture relied on as teaching universal restoration; and the expression of such a judgment is offered in these pages. But here arises a formidable practical difficulty. If the progress of the argument is to depend on the reader's accepting in every instance the proposed exposition, further advance must be impossible. To impose such a condition would be unreasonable and unjust. All that is essential here is to show that the passages in question bear an explanation wholly different from that which these writers put upon them; and this at least has been accomplished. Indeed, it is sufficiently established by the admitted fact that such an explanation has been given by the overwhelming majority of theologians in every age. The advocates of universalism have been content to plead that the surface teaching of these Scriptures is in favour of their views: they must go further, and oust the alternative meanings assigned to them by the scholarship of Christendom. But this they have never attempted to do.

This position is not assumed to avoid the necessity of explaining the passages referred to. The reader will find in the Appendix a full exposition of every text on which the universalist relies to prove his doctrine. This exegesis is offered in acknowledgment of the obligation to explain these Scriptures, but it is dismissed to the Appendix as a protest against the assumption that the acceptance of it is vital to the argument. It is not vital. On the contrary, having thus cleared the ground, we shall now suppose for the sake of argument,—and it is only on that ground the admission can be made,—that the meaning of these passages is doubtful, and proceed on this assumption to discuss the question in the light of great foundation truths.

---

1. Do not such arguments as are here alluded to remind us of a king's baby children in the royal nursery discussing the fate of some notorious criminal, and deciding that

they knew their father so well as to be assured he could not and would not sign a death-warrant?
2. Therefore, these passages tell against the view they are cited in support of, by weakening the popular argument based on the supposition that the saved will be an insignificant minority.
3. Acts iii. 21- 24.

CHAPTER 5
"THE WIDER HOPE."

The volumes noticed in preceding pages have not been selected at random. Their respective authors are representative men, the acknowledged champions of "the wider hope"; and their books, when read together, may be taken as a full and exhaustive statement of the doctrine. The omissions therefore common to them all are ominously significant. Where, for example, do they offer us any reasonable explanation of such passages as the following? "The Lord Jesus shall be revealed from heaven with His mighty angels in flaming fire, taking vengeance on them that know not God, and that obey not the gospel of our Lord Jesus Christ; who shall be punished with everlasting destruction from the presence of the Lord."[1] How can such language be reconciled with the dogma of universal restoration? Is it credible that any one holding that dogma could use such words?[2]

But there are other omissions of a still more serious kind, and, for our present purpose, far more embarrassing. We may agree to exclude from view any number of "isolated texts," but how can common ground be reached save in the acknowledgment of truths such as the righteousness of God, the grace of God, the "resurrection of the dead, both of the just and of the unjust," and the great judgment which is to close the history of Adam's race?[3] It is on this ground alone we can consent to discuss the question.

It will, therefore, be taken as admitted that the many die unsaved, and that these shall be raised from the dead, and shall stand before God in judgment, and be remitted to punishment for their sins. The question here is not of what may be called the *providential* consequences of sin, the results which in God's moral government follow the violation of His laws. Neither is it a question of corrective discipline to purge and train the penitent. There is no need of a Day of Judgment to apportion punishment in either of these senses: the one follows the sin by unchanging law; the other belongs entirely to the Father's house. The final punishment of the lost will be the consequence of a judicial sentence.

Such punishment, therefore, must be the

penalty due to their sins; else it were unrighteous to impose it. If, then, the lost are ultimately to be saved, it must be either because they shall have satisfied the penalty; or else through redemption—that is, because Christ has borne that penalty for them. But if sinners can be saved by satisfying Divine justice in enduring the penalty due to sin, Christ need not have died. If, on the other hand, the redeemed may yet be doomed, though ordained to eternal life in Christ, themselves to endure the penalty for sin, the foundations of our faith are destroyed. It is not, I repeat, the providential or disciplinary, but the *penal* consequences of sin, which follow the judgment. We can therefore understand how the sinner may escape his doom through his debt being paid vicariously, or we can (*in theory*, at all events) admit that he may be discharged on payment personally of "the uttermost farthing"; but that the sinner should be made to pay a portion of his debt, and then released because some one else had paid the whole before he was remitted to punishment at all,—this is absolutely inconsistent with both righteousness and grace.

But as the advocates of the "larger hope" seem to ignore the penal element in punishment, they would probably urge that this is satisfied by redemption, and that the sufferings of the lost will be essentially of a disciplinary kind. All who know much of the darker side of human nature would probably agree that the poetry indulged in about sinners being purified in aeonian fire would not bear translation into simple prose. The idea of reformation by punishment has been generally abandoned by all who have had experience of criminals and crime. But passing that by, it may be answered, first, that such a view is incompatible with the language of Scripture. "Wrath," "vengeance," "destruction" are not words that express parental chastisement. But as these writers must be supposed to have some reasonable explanation of such Scriptures, it may be answered, secondly, that if their doctrines be sound, it is in the *intermediate* state that suffering would produce these results; and if a further non-penal "punishment" is to be inflicted after the resurrection and the judgment, this must be in order to coerce the sinner to submission.

It might be asked, in passing, what value can possibly attach to a repentance wrung in this way from unwilling souls? and, moreover, if hell and the lake of fire shall produce results so blessed, how can it be evil to warn men of the coming horrors? If the reality shall be so beneficial, surely the fear of its terrors can work only good; and the more appalling the description, the greater will be the effect produced.

Thirdly, the question arises whether regeneration, and the need of it, have any place in the theology of the advocates of these doctrines. Divine "chastening" may produce "the peaceable fruit of righteousness" in those who are already "sons"; but to hold that punishment is necessary either as a preparation for, or a completion of, "the new birth," is to deny the plainest teaching of Scripture.

Again, it may be asked still more definitely, what room is there in this scheme for the day of judgment? The believer "cometh not into judgment,' just because, for him, the penalty of sin has been borne, the judicial question settled, in the death of Christ; and if this be true for all, the judgment of "the great assize" becomes an anachronism and an impossibility.[4]

This suggests another difficulty. The sceptic who demands, "How are the dead raised up, and with what body do they come?" is branded as a fool. But is it folly to inquire, How shall the lost be translated, and with what body shall *they* come? And let it be kept prominently in view that the resurrection precedes the judgment. They who have part in the "resurrection of life" shall bear "the image of the heavenly." "When He shall appear we shall be like Him," is the amazing statement of the Scripture. But in contrast with the "resurrection of life" there is also the "resurrection of judgment." Why then call up the evil body at all, unless it be the *final* condition of the lost? It is not the *body* that repents, or believes, or turns to God; and, as already urged, if torment could be remedial, it is in the intermediate state it would be efficacious. The conclusion is inevitable that the body is reunited to the soul in order that the sinner may in the body in which he sinned endure the punishment his sins deserve.

And this is the plain teaching of Scripture. But when we are asked to believe that, after the ages of his torment shall have passed, the sinner will be translated in a new and heavenly body, to share the peace and blessedness of the redeemed, we part company with Scripture altogether. It is not a question here of "isolated texts," but of the great foundation truths of Christianity. If these torments be necessary, where are the triumphs of redemption through the Cross? If unnecessary, what becomes of the love of God? If sinners can reach heaven through the lake of fire, redemption is but "a short cut" to the same goal to which the broad way ultimately leads. Christ need not have died, or, at all events, far too much has been said about His death. Will they who thus reach heaven through "aeonian torments" have much appreciation of the brief agonies of Calvary?[5]

To recapitulate. The question is not whether the destiny of all be fixed at death, but whether the judgment of the great day be irreversible and final. Not whether God be a Saviour to all men, but whether all men shall be saved, including those who reject the Saviour. Not whether Christ be a propitiation for the whole world, but whether the whole world shall share the pardon, including those who despise the propitiation. There is not a single text of Scripture which unequivocally teaches that all men shall in fact be saved; there are many which declare in the plainest terms that the judgment-doom of the lost is final. The dogma of universalism depends solely on the assumption that the love of God is incompatible with the perdition of ungodly men—an assumption which may rest entirely on our ignorance, and which, moreover, when worked out to its legitimate results, undermines Christianity altogether It is blind folly to abandon the doctrine of eternal punishment because of difficulties which surround it, and then to take refuge in a belief which is beset with difficulties far more hopeless. If, then, there be no other escape, we fall back unhesitatingly upon the faith of the Church in all ages. But another alternative remains : punishment may be final, and yet it may not be endless.

---

1. 2 Thess. i. 7-9.
2. The author last referred to, with the candour which characterises him, says, "I confess I cannot perfectly explain all these texts."
3. The respective schemes of the first two writers seem inconsistent with belief in the "resurrection of judgment." The third writer dismisses it thus "Of the details of this resurrection, of the nature and state of the bodies of the judged,—*if indeed bodies in which there is any image of a man*, and therefore of God, then are given to them,—and of the scene of judgment, very little is said in Scripture."

The meaning of this is clearly that the body given at the "resurrection of judgment" is merely a temporary clothing for the soul, and that the soul shall not be reunited to the heavenly and final body until after punishment shall have been endured.

4. The language of John v. 24 is explicit. It is not that the believer "shall not come into condemnation" as the A. V. renders it, but that he *cometh into judgment* . This statement must not be made to clash with Rom. xiv. 10, and 2 Cor. v. 10, which relate to the judgment of the saved. At the resurrection the believer shall appear in "the image of the heavenly,"—"we shall be like Him." That is to say, his destiny is not only fixed but declared at the resurrection. For him, therefore, the judgment will be on that basis: it will be a matter of reward or loss, not of life or death. As Heb. ix. 27, 28 teaches, the cross of Christ and His glorious advent are, for the believer, the correlatives of death and judgment.

Matt. xxv. 31-46 describes a session of judgment for living nations on earth, and has no bearing on the special point here raised.

5. I have already shown that of the books quoted supra two practically ignore redemption. I desire to be perfectly fair, and I have searched the volume last noticed (which was the first written, and inspired the other two) to find a warrant for clearing the author from this reproach; but I cannot. And if such an one as he is betrayed into such language as the following, it may be taken as certain that the views he advocates are inconsistent with Christian doctrine. "What does he say here" (he writes, quoting Rev, xxi. 5-8), "but that all things shall be made new, though in the way to this the fearful and unbelieving must pass the lake of fire? . . . *The saints have died with Christ,* not only to the elements of this world, but also to sin, that is the dark spirit world . . . *The ungodly have not so died to sin*. At the death of the body, therefore, and still more when they are raised to judgment, because their spirit yet lives, they are still within the limits of that dark and fiery world, the life of which has been and is the life of their spirit. *To get*

out of this world there is but one way, death. Not the first, for that is passed, but the second death."

The italics are my own. The extraordinary mysticism which pervades this makes it difficult to fix its meaning, but I am unable to understand it if it does not teach that *the lake of fire* (the second death) *is to the impenitent what the cross of Christ is to the believer.*

CHAPTER 6
WHAT IS LIFE?

To some the doctrine of endless punishment seems to present no difficulty. Others again are so decided in rejecting it that if only the dogma of universal restoration be discredited, they are prepared at once to adopt what seems the only alternative, the extermination of the wicked. For the one class these pages can have but a speculative interest. For the other, their practical importance ceases at the point already reached. But it is only the superficial who can ignore the difficulties that beset the problem which still claims discussion. And, moreover, the rejection of the "wider hope," just because it narrows the inquiry, deepens immensely its importance and solemnity. When our escape from pressing difficulties depends upon a single door, more care is needed than when we supposed we had a choice.

Two questions lie across the threshold of the inquiry: What is the meaning of the Greek word *aiōnios*? and, Does man by nature possess immortality? If, to borrow a military term, we can *mask* these difficulties, instead of delaying to settle them, we shall avoid an almost interminable controversy.

It is maintained by some that *aiōnios* means age-long, and nothing else; but these admit that all men have an age-long existence.[1] Others, again, contend that the word means everlasting; but these insist that all men shall exist for ever. In either case, therefore, the solemn language of Scripture, which declares aeonian life to be the peculiar blessing of the believer, loses all its significance, unless we understand the word to describe the *quality* of the life, and not duration merely.[2] We must conclude, then, that in all such passages the emphasis is upon *life*, and it is here our attention should be concentrated.

This brings in the second question. The word immortality occurs but thrice in the New Testament. In one of these passages St. Paul declares that God "only hath immortality": in the other, the believer is twice described as a mortal who is destined to "put on immortality." It certainly seems strange, therefore, that any who profess to follow Holy Writ should contend for the expression "the immortality of the soul" more especially as man's spiritual condition by nature is described as *death* and not life? What then is life?

Here science can tell us nothing. If we seek the *origin* of life, Reason answers in one word, GOD. Let the existence of life be taken for granted, and then, no doubt, evolution will offer to account for all the varied *forms* of life in the world.[3] But until science can get rid of God, the theory is unnecessary, and therefore unphilosophical. It is the old question, Does the hen come from the egg, or the egg from the hen? If science could account for the egg, it would be entitled to put that first. But as we are shut up to believe in a Creator, it is more reasonable, and therefore more philosophical, to assume that He created the hen. This, of course, is apart from Revelation, which, for the Christian, puts the question at rest for ever.

And science can tell as little about life itself as about its origin. It has its definitions, doubtless, but these either assume or ignore precisely what they profess to give us. "Correspondence with an environment" is the latest and most vaunted.[4] The table on which this paper lies would soon be destroyed by the action of fire or water, but it corresponds with its actual environment. If however we infer that the table has life, we shall be told that a dead thing cannot correspond with an environment at all; it must have a *principle of life* to render correspondence possible. It appears, then, that the vaunted definition deals merely with phenomena; whereas it is life considered *essentially*, not in its manifestations, that concerns us here. The fact is, biology can tell us about *bios*, but about *zoe* (ζωή) it knows absolutely nothing.

Some will be impatient at a disquisition about life. To them it seems the simplest thing possible : life is the opposite of death, and thus the whole matter is settled. But this is to shelve the difficulty, not to settle it. And the question is of extreme importance here. If we are justified in taking life to mean existence, then death is the termination of existence, and we are within reach of the goal we seek. But this must be proved, and not taken for granted.

Our word "life" has to do duty for the two Greek words just cited. And each of these has several different meanings and shades of meaning. As already indicated, *zoe* is life in its principle, life intrinsic; *bios*, life in its manifestations, life extrinsic. But there is more in it than this. *Bios* may signify the *period* or duration of life; secondly, one's "living," or the *means* of life; and thirdly, the *manner* of life. An example of each of these phases of meaning will be found among the eleven passages in which the word is used in the New Testament.[5]

From this last use of the word, as the manner of life, there is often an ethical sense attaching to it, and this is expressed in classical Greek exclusively by bios; in Scripture exclusively by *zoe*[6]. Zoe, again, is sometimes the equivalent of *bios*, as expressing the *means* of life; and our translators have taken it in Luke xvi. 25 as meaning the *period* of life. It is also used to express the final blessedness of the redeemed[7] or the sphere in which it will be enjoyed; the present condition of the believer, who, it is said, "is passed from death into life,"[8] and finally and emphatically, the *principle* of life. The often-repeated statement that the believer "hath life" does not mean merely that he is in a state of blessedness; he is in life, but more than this, he has life in him. This is clear from the contrast, "No murderer hath eternal life abiding in him;"[9] or as the Lord said to the Jews, "Ye have no life in you."[10]

But it will be urged, perhaps, that in all this the simple and plain meaning of life as equivalent to existence has been ignored. But can life be thus taken as a synonym for existence at all? If so, then the table has life, for it certainly exists. But the definition may possibly be amended by saying *conscious* existence: the table has not *that*. No; neither had the tree the table was made of, though it certainly had life; neither has a man in a swoon. The fact is, and it must in fairness be conceded, that "life" does not admit of any such definition. If we want its ordinary meaning we must turn to a dictionary, and there we shall find that life is that state of an organised being in which its functions are or may be performed. Death, then, is the antithesis of this. An organism is dead when its vital functions have ceased absolutely and permanently.

It has been denied that reason can tell us anything certainly of a life after death, and it will be here assumed that it cannot. As we have revelation to guide us, the admission may be freely made. Death came into the world by sin, and it is the penalty of sin. If, then, we might conclude that death puts an end to the existence of all save those who receive eternal life in Christ, the whole question would be settled. But the teaching of Scripture is explicit, that while death is a great crisis in human existence, it is not, as with the brutes, its goal. "It is appointed unto men once to die, and after death the judgment." Such is the testimony of Scripture. But the penalty of sin must follow the judgment, and not precede it. The death, therefore, which is the penalty of sin, cannot be "natural death."

The same conclusion will be arrived at from considering the warning given to Adam in Eden. It was not merely that on eating of the tree of knowledge he should become mortal. The word was, "In the day that thou eatest thereof thou shalt surely die." Is it not clear, then, that the ordinary meaning of death is not its primary or its deepest meaning? And further, as the crisis which we call death is merely a change of condition, why should we suppose that the death which follows the judgment will be anything else?

These difficulties are nothing to shallow declaimers against everlasting punishment, but every serious opponent of the doctrine has recognised that they are of vital moment. The advocate of "conditional immortality" is bound, not only to notice them, but to answer them fully and completely.

---

1. Whether this be natural to the race, or the result of redemption, makes no difference to my argument.
2. I say advisedly, *"not duration merely."* "Eternal life," Dr. Westcott writes, "is not an endless duration of being in time, but being of which time is not a measure." And again, it "is beyond the limitations of time; it belongs to the being of God." (*Epistles of St. John*, pp. 205 and 207.) But surely endless duration is implied in this, though it is not the main element in it. I do not stop to discuss wherein the above statement differs from Mr. Maurice's view.
3. "Of the causes which have led to the origination of living matter, then, it may be said that we know absolutely nothing. But postulating the existence of living matter endowed with that power of hereditary transmission, and with that tendency to vary which is found in all such matter, Mr. Darwin has shown good reasons for believing that the interaction between living matter and surrounding conditions, which results in the survival of the fittest, is sufficient to account for the gradual evolution of plants and animals from their simplest to their most complicated forms."—Prof. Huxley, *Encyclopedia Britannica* (9th ed.), "Biology," vol. iii., p. 68
4. Professor Drummont is enthusiastic over this definition of life in his charming book of parables—it is earnestly to

be hoped that *Natural Law* will not be taken in any more serious light. The fact is, that having been betrayed into bracketing together Herbert Spencer and "Jesus Christ" as authors of rival definitions of "eternal life" (p. 203), his hobby ran away with him. "Through all these centuries" (he declares) "revealed religion had this doctrine to itself." "It has been reserved for modern biology at once to defend and illuminate this central truth of the Christian faith." This, although he has rightly stated at p. 146 that "no definition of life that has yet appeared can be said to be even approximately correct"; and as he goes on to aver, at p. 228, that "to say that life is a correspondence, is only to express the partial truth .... there is a principle of life." And yet he says, at p. 215, "All life consists *essentially* in correspondence with various environments." Moreover, the words of our Blessed Lord in John xvii. 3, as read in the original, cannot be taken as a definition of life, any more than in John iv. 34. He gave a definition of His food. Without attempting to discuss that crux of the grammarians as to the telic force of ἵνα, we may assume that the particle does not introduce a definition.
5. Matt. xii. 44; Luke viii. 14, 43, xv. 12, 30, xxi. 4; I Tim. ii. 2; 2 Tim. ii. 4; i Peter iv. 3; I John ii. 16, iii. 17.
6. Trench's Synonyms.
7. Matt, xviii. 8, 9, xxv. 46; Mark ix. 43, 45, x. 30, *ex. gr.*
8. John v. 24; I John iii. 14.
9. I John iii. 15.
10. John vi. 53.

CHAPTER 7
"ETERNAL LIFE IN CHRIST."

In the wide and increasing field of literature on this question there is one volume which enjoys a well-deserved pre-eminence. It has now been forty years before the public, and during that time it has been subjected to the severest criticism. In the light of that criticism it was rewritten eleven years ago, and since then it has been again revised with the most scrupulous care. Its pages are characterised by reverent piety, competent scholarship, and intellectual power of no mean order; and in fact it is justly deemed the standard work on the subject of which it treats. Every statement it contains has evidently been weighed, and seeming omissions will be accounted for, not by the author's ignorance of anything which others have written, but because in his judgment their arguments are either unfair or unwise. To this book we turn for the most complete and favourable answer possible to the difficulties which have just been stated.

The author frankly acknowledges that the views he opposes are "supported by the general authority of nearly all Christendom for at least fourteen centuries"; and that they have been accepted by "instructed divines who are to be counted by hundreds of thousands, belonging to all Churches, in every successive century of Christianity." Nevertheless he opposes them. "According to the Bible" (he declares) "man is essentially a complex being, consisting of body and soul;" not a soul without a body, any more than a body without a soul. Adam was such a being. The warning, "In the day that thou eatest thereof thou shalt surely die," implied not *liability* to "temporal death," still less to endless misery, but death itself, "the utter destruction of Adam's nature as a man," and that literally on the very day of his sin. The threatening "was intended to signify a literal, immediate, and final dissolution of the nature of Adam as a man; his death in the ordinary sense of the word, without any reference whatever to the state, or even to the survival, of the spirit beyond." "The humanity is the living organism, including body and soul. When that complex organism is dissolved the man is no more." The death, therefore, threatened to Adam, and which he was to suffer on the very day of his sin, *was the absolute extinction of his being.*

Such, moreover, the author maintains, as he is bound to maintain, is "death in the ordinary sense of the word." And further, "this death was 'the curse of the law'; not merely of the Mosaic law, but of that law under which Adam was created at first, and of which the thunders of Sinai were a second manifestation."

But whatever may be doubtful, this at least is certain, that no such doom has in fact fallen upon the sinner. How can this enigma be explained? The author solves it by the one word *Redemption.* "From the moment of the sin" (he tells us) "the action of Redemption began at once to unfold itself." "This survival of the soul we attribute exclusively (with Delitzsch) to the operation of Redemption." Such a survival "is contrary to the original intention of God in the curse of death threatened at first to Adam in Paradise;" it is "of the nature of a miraculous or abnormal provision, arising out of the economy of redemption, with a view to future resurrection." And "the sentence of death is postponed, not repealed." Absolute extinction of his being is therefore the sinner's doom.[1]

It is impossible to exaggerate the importance and solemnity of these statements. The whole controversy is thus narrowed to a single issue. If the death which is the penalty of sin be the extinction of the sinner's being, the doctrine of conditional immortality is a Divine truth. If, on the other hand, that death be merely a changed condition of existence, the doctrine is a sheer delusion, and an error of the grossest and most dangerous kind. As, therefore, the result of our judgment on this question is so unspeakably solemn, no amount of earnestness or care can be excessive in considering it.

First, then, as already shown, the definition here given of death cannot be accepted for a moment. The extinction of being would certainly *imply death*; but death itself, in its ordinary sense, means nothing but the change in which the performance of vital functions ceases, or else the condition of the organism which has suffered that change. The thought is the same whether the subject be a man or a brute. If it be asked whether in either case there is a soul that survives, this is a new question the answer to which is not involved in the thought of death. When the Roman soldiers, after breaking the legs of the crucified thieves, came to the body of the Blessed Lord and pronounced Him dead, they meant precisely the same thing as if they had been dealing with a bullock or a sheep.

The author is right, therefore, in asserting that in the thought of death there is no reference to the survival of a spirit beyond. But he is wholly wrong in assuming that death is inconsistent with such a survival. And yet this is implied in his statement that "the man is no more"; for if it means merely that a disembodied soul ought not to be described as a *Man*, the proposition relates only to the use of words, and is of no practical importance here.

The question may be stated thus:

What has become of Balaam and of the beast he rode upon? The answer is, They are dead, But, it is again asked, was death the end of their existence? We have agreed to put Reason out of court on this point, so we turn to Scripture, and Scripture tells us that death was the end of the beast, but not of the man. Does not this decide the matter, then? By no means, the author replies, because Balaam's survival is "a miraculous or abnormal provision, arising out of the economy of redemption." What grounds are there for this statement? Absolutely none; it is a mere theory put forward arbitrarily, and without a shadow of proof, in order to avoid a difficulty in which the author finds himself entangled by the view he takes of death, which again is equally arbitrary and baseless, and which, moreover, assumes the very thing he is attempting to prove.

The controversy turns upon what is called the "natural immortality" of the soul—that is, that apart from Divine interference, and by the law of its being, the human soul will continue to exist for ever. The advocate of conditional immortality undertakes to prove the opposite of this proposition.

But how does he proceed? As the foundation of his argument he puts forward a definition of death which covertly implies, and that without proof, the precise conclusion which he is bound to establish; and then, finding himself confronted by plain facts of which Revelation testifies, he disposes of those facts by a new theory about redemption. Moreover, the necessity for this theory arises solely from the error of the position he has taken up; and this being so, the silence of Scripture is a sufficient reason for rejecting it. If the survival of the soul depended on redemption, it is incredible that the doctrine could not be plainly revealed. And further, unless the sentence upon Adam was an arbitrary one, the theory fails to account for the facts. If death is the consequence of sin, Satan and his angels had already come under death, and as they have no part in redemption, their survival cannot be accounted for by redemption.

Mark what all this involves. According to the threatening, we are told, the judgment upon Adam was the extinction of his being, and that too upon the day of his sin. Yet he lived nine hundred and thirty years, and when at last death overtook him his soul survived. We must conclude, therefore, that God threatened him with a doom which He had no intention of inflicting. The only thing certain about it is that Satan was entirely in the right when he met the Divine warning by a flat denial, and declared, "Ye shall *not* surely die." It behoves us peremptorily to reject such a supposition, no matter what the rejection of it may involve, and to insist that whatever the threatened death implied, it came upon Adam in the day of his sin.

Certain it is that a change took place in his condition and relationships with God. If even from the standpoint of fallen humanity the loss of virtue is deemed worse than death, how unspeakably terrible must have been that first plunge from innocence into sin! Death, we are told, is the dissolution of the complex organism which constitutes the human integer; in other words, it is the breaking up of the *Man*, the separation of soul and body. What word then can more fitly express that far more awful crisis, the separation of the creature from his God? This and nothing less than this surely is death in its fullest, deepest sense.

This same conclusion may be reached in another way. The believer "hath passed out of death into life."[2] The condition of the sinner, therefore, by nature is death. How and when did mankind come into this state? The answer is clear, By the fall of Adam. To urge that every sinner is dead by reason of his own trespasses and sins is only to confirm the correctness of the reply, by establishing that sin results in death. The word "death" expresses both the crisis and the condition into which it introduces the sinner. In the latter sense, natural death is a condition of existence in separation from the body, and spiritual death is a condition of existence in separation from God.

But as this would be decisive, it is met again by a bold rejection of the whole doctrine of spiritual death. We are told that the expression is "without example in apostolic usage," and that when Scripture describes the unregenerate as dead, the language is figurative, and "the figure is in the *tense*," meaning "they are certain to die, because they are under sentence of destruction." In answer to this, first, the need of the term *spiritual* death arises solely from using the term *natural* death. It is adopted, not of necessity, but only for clearness and brevity. Secondly, it cannot be admitted that there is any figure here at all, for, as already urged, the ordinary meaning of death is not necessarily its primary meaning. And, thirdly, the author's statement is only a repetition of his invariable *petitio principii*. He must prove, and not take for granted, that death means extinction of being.

The last remark applies with full force to the author's argument on St. Paul's reference to death in the 5th chapter of Romans. Allow him to assume what he undertakes to prove, and his argument is unanswerable; but hold him to the proof of it, and it falls to pieces. The apostle desires to prove that Adam sinned as federal head of the race, involving his posterity in the consequences of his sin; and to establish this, he appeals to the fact that death reigned even at a time when, and over persons in respect of whom, there was no question of actual transgression, death being admittedly one of the consequences of the Eden sin.[3]

Further, we are told that the death with which Adam was threatened was also the curse of the law, "literal death," that is, implying destruction in the sense in which these writers use the word. To this it may be answered, first, that here again the argument moves in the usual vicious circle, that which is to be proved being taken for granted; and, secondly, that the statement confounds the curse with the consequences of the curse. The same word, "cursed," is applied to the law-breaker, to the serpent in Eden, and to the ground condemned to bring forth thorns and thistles.[4] In no case was it the end of their existence, but the ban under which existence was to continue. True it is the law-breaker was put to death, because in the Commonwealth of Israel the sinner who came under the Divine curse was utterly outlawed. The death was inflicted by man, and therefore the offender might escape it. In fact, during the apostacy of the nation escape was the almost universal rule; but the Divine curse upon the law-breaker was none the less certain and inexorable.

One point more remains, and it is incomparably the most important. Whatever be the death which is the penalty of sin, that death was endured by Christ. This at least is a statement which none will gainsay. If then death be "the destruction" (that is, the *extinction*) "of the life of humanity," "*death for ever*, dissolution without hope of the resurrection," did *this* death befall the blessed Lord? One might have supposed that the mere statement of the question would have been enough; but it would seem that the advocate of "conditional immortality" is prepared to defend his position no matter what the cost. He not only meets the question, but answers it as follows, by an uncompromising affirmative:

"When Christ died, He was, *as a man*, destroyed." "When the curse had taken effect upon the manhood"—of Jesus—"it was still open to the Divine Inhabitant, absorbing the Spirit into His own essence, to restore the 'destroyed temple' from its ruins, and taking possession of it in virtue of His Divinity (not legally, as a man), to raise it up on the third day." Or, still more plainly in borrowed words which the author adopts, "It was the life of man,—a life common to Him with those He died to redeem, that expired on the tree : but the life He now enjoys is the life of God. Of justice He takes back no part of the penalty He had paid. It is to the power of His eternal Godhead alone that He owes His resurrection from the dead."

Hitherto this argument has been conducted with calmness, but at this point the Christian may well exclaim, "With such a theme 'twere treason to be calm." What is the cost at which the advocates of "conditional immortality" here defend their position? First, as to their own consistency. They begin by insisting that the body is so essentially *the man*, that when the human organism is dissolved *the man* is no more;[5] but when driven to it by the exigencies of an argument based on error, and marked throughout by fallacy, they end by assuming that the body is no part of the man at all, so that when the blessed Lord gave up His human soul He perfectly satisfied the death which claimed *the man* as its due. We are told that "if Jesus had been the Son of David only, He could not legally have risen from the dead." But why not? If the resurrection was merely a transcendental trick, what did it matter whether the corpse which lay in Joseph's tomb had *formerly* been animated by Divine life or not? The *human* life had been "destroyed," and all claims of law having thus been met, God could of course reanimate that body. On this theory, indeed, what need was there for redemption at all? By a like piece of chicanery he who had the power of death might have been cheated of his due in every child of Adam.[6]

But the question is not whether the Lord could have been raised from the dead had He been only the Son of David. The real question is, whether, in fact, He was raised from the dead only as Son of God. Perchance that strange admonition to Timothy had reference to some such heresy as this, even in the infant Church, "Remember that Jesus Christ was raised from the dead, of the seed of

David, according to my gospel."[7] The whole argument of the apostle in the fifteenth chapter of First Corinthians is based upon the fact that Christ was raised from the dead *as man*. The words are, "Since *by man* came death, *by man* came also the resurrection of the dead." Therefore it is that in His resurrection He "became the firstfruits of them that slept." The firstfruits must of necessity be a part of the harvest; and such was indeed "the last *Adam*," "the second *man*, the Lord from heaven."

Christianity is based upon the very truth which is here denied. Paradise regained is a poet's dream, but it has no place in the theology of the New Testament. The scheme of redemption is not to restore the first Adam to the place he lost by sin, as federal head of the old creation; but, closing his history for ever in the Cross of Calvary, to unite the redeemed of the fallen race under the Second Adam as federal head of the new creation. The one Mediator is THE MAN Christ Jesus."[8] "It is as *Son of Man* He took His place at the right hand of God."[9] When the Son of Man shall come in His glory,[10] and all the holy angels with Him, then shall He sit upon the throne of His glory." It is "because He is the Son of Man" that the Father "has given Him authority to execute judgment."[11]

1. I shall be told probably that the author does not speak of death as "extinction of being." This is true, and it is a signal proof of the skill with which his argument is conducted. Other writers had used the expression, and their position had been easily stormed in consequence; so he avoids it. But his argument *implies* it; and without it it has no force whatever. Therefore I have taken the liberty of *expressing* it.
2. John v. 24, R. V. j cf. I John iii. 14.
3. Some advocates of conditional immortality do not admit this; but one must really draw a line somewhere as to turning aside to prove facts and truths accepted by all Christendom.
4. Gen. iii. 14, 17; Deut. xxvii. 15, 16, 17, 18, 19, 20, etc. The same word *āh-rar* is used in all these passages.
5. According to the author already quoted, "Both the law and the Gospel deal with man as an integer, consisting of body and soul. *The death incurred by sin was the destruction of this complex humanity.*"
6. This same writer avers that the survival of the soul at death is to establish continuity of personality for judgment. "If no spirit survived, it might be truly said that a wholly *new* being was then created to suffer for the offences of another long passed away." So we say if the *Man* Christ Jesus did not rise from the dead a wholly *new* being was called to life at the resurrection.
7. 2 Tim. ii. 8.
8. I Tim. ii. 5.
9. Acts vii. 56
10. Matt. xxv. 31.
11. John v. 27.

CHAPTER 8
ANNIHILATION.

The natural immortality of man, we are told, is a theory of heathen philosophers, engrafted upon Christianity in post-apostolic days. Man is a dying creature, destined by the operation of natural laws to pass out of existence unless he receive eternal life in Christ. It is admitted, however, that the lost shall be raised from the dead by Divine power in order that in the body they may be judged and punished for their sins. In other words, creatures who are doomed by the law of their nature to decay and pass out of being altogether, are not only kept in existence, but recalled to active life in resurrection, solely in order that increased capacities for enduring torment may be added to the horrors of their doom. Not even the coarse hell of medieaval ignorance is more revolting, more incredible than this; and yet these views are held and taught on the plea that God is a God of love!

But Scripture plainly teaches that the destruction of the wicked—whatever destruction means—is the result, not of natural law, but of Divine judgment. When we read that "the wages of sin is death," we are to understand extinction of being. Now we know as a matter of experience and of fact that death often entails much antecedent suffering; but on the same ground we know also that this is purely accidental. Death does not necessarily involve any suffering whatever. If human law sentences a criminal to imprisonment, it consigns him to misery in many forms; but if it decrees his death, it scrupulously guards him from every kind of suffering save the necessary rigour of confinement. Nor is it that he is dismissed to receive his punishment from God. Our English law at least is not so cruel. The conventional language of the death sentence concludes with a prayer for Divine mercy on the condemned, and a minister of religion is appointed to attend him in his cell and on the scaffold. The last words that fall upon his ears are words that tell of pardon and a life beyond the grave. If capital punishment were abolished the public would probably insist on the free use of the lash for grave and brutal crimes; but how degraded would be the community which would decree a criminal's death, and yet torture him up to the very hour of his execution![1]

Now let us test the argument in the light of the inevitable admissions. If what we call death were the end of the sinner, all would be plain. But it is admitted that the lost dead are to be raised for judgment, and in their bodies subjected to punitive suffering for their sins; and that this suffering, though limited in duration, shall yet be terrible. Is not this open to every objection on the ground of reason and sentiment which is urged against the "orthodox faith"? If there be some awful necessity, unexplained to us, why the sinner should continue to exist, we can understand that there may be a like necessity for future punishment; but if there be no such necessity, what is it but torturing helpless, hopeless victims who might at once be put out of misery, for extinction is their doom?

The author already quoted as the champion of conditional immortality is far too keen a reasoner to overlook this difficulty. He has met it boldly by disclaiming the belief that ages of suffering are to precede that destruction, "thus parting company with Scripture altogether. In his view the sufferings of the lost in the final state will be merely such as shall necessarily accompany their "death"; and we must read this statement in the light of the undoubted fact that *no suffering* whatever is involved in death when inflicted without cruelty. Is there then to be *no* suffering for sin? In reply the author will tell us that "the spirit may suffer *in Hades* for the sins of a lifetime." But what then becomes of the statement that at death *the man* is no more? If "the spirit" carries with it the moral guilt of life's sins and a capacity of suffering for those sins, *this* is the personality, this is "the man." Moreover, according to this theory, the amount of a sinner's punishment depends, not on the character of his sin, but on the epoch at which he lived on earth. In the antediluvian sinner it is measured by thousands of years : whereas for the awful Christ-rejecter of the last days it will be briefer than for all the rest; because Hades is to be cast into the lake of fire, and the lake of fire is absolute extinction of being.

But the suffering in Hades precedes the judgment. What room is there then for judgment at all? The object of the day of judgment is to fix the guilt and apportion the punishment of each, and it becomes but an idle pageant if all alike are to be hurried to a swift and common doom. To answer that its purpose will be to separate the redeemed from the impenitent is to ignore some of the plainest teaching of Scripture. *That* division will be manifested in and by the resurrection, for the redeemed shall be raised in "the image of the heavenly," and such are not to come into the judgment.[2] And what possible purpose can there be in this view for the resurrection of the lost? We are asked to believe that God not only maintains them in existence by miraculous interference, but that He puts forth His mighty power to raise them from the dead, solely and altogether for a magnificent display of wrath in annihilating them.

But apart from the essential incredibility of such a theory, we must reject it as opposed to the plain testimony of Scripture. We turn, therefore, to seek the explanation from another writer, whose published sermons on this subject are held in high repute by all believers in conditional immortality. He will tell us that the doom of the impenitent "will *not* be a simple act of annihilation, but a process of destruction. The fire of God's wrath will not consume them at once, but they will be tormented in it day and night for the ages of ages that they have yet to live." "Many or few stripes will be inflicted, according to each one's deserts, while in every case it will end in the final loss of life as the necessary consequence of not being in Christ." In terms at least this is consistent with the language of Scripture, and therefore it claims consideration.

Does not this suggest the inquiry how suicide is to be prevented in the lake of fire? God must put forth His miraculous power to keep in being the victims of His wrath, until the last of the "many or few stripes" which each one deserves shall have been inflicted! Disguise it as we may, the fact is obvious that in this theory the annihilation of the lost is God's act of mercy to close their suffering. It is impious to suppose that their release could be delayed wantonly and cruelly. The delay, therefore, must be due to the righteous necessity of exacting the full meed of punishment the sin of each deserves. Why then should a God "Who is willing that all men should be saved," not let the damned pass from the scene of torment to some place of rest, instead of putting forth His power to annihilate them?

Further, if annihilation be the penalty of sin, then, as already shown, Christ has not borne that penalty. If it be a term of suffering, from which annihilation gives release, redemption is seriously depreciated. This view is beset by difficulties akin to those which led us to abandon. the "wider hope," and in addition to these it presents a difficulty of another and far graver kind. As the writer last quoted puts it, the punishment "will be inflicted according to each one's deserts," the annihilation will be "the necessary consequence of not being in Christ." We are thus asked to believe in a God who puts forth His power solely to keep His creatures in existence until "the uttermost farthing" of penalty has been exacted, and who then, when every question of righteous claim is settled, and love might pity and save, turns away to leave them to their fate. And this, too, on the plea that God is a God of love!

Either there exists a righteous necessity to punish sin, or there does not. If there be no such necessity, then all punitive suffering is inflicted wantonly and cruelly. If, on the other hand, sin must be punished, how and when is that punishment to cease? The hell of the Bible is consistent with Divine love, but the hell of the annihilationist is more horrible even than the conventional hell of popular theology. Is such a hell to make men righteous and holy—this awful pit of shrieking, cursing men, made desperate by despair, and maddened by the knowledge that if God would only let them alone their torment would cease for ever? These sins of the lake of fire, are they to go unpunished? Does the quality of guilt depend on the atmosphere of earth, and not on the unchanging laws of God?

The only difference between the hell of the annihilationist and the coarse hell of medieval theologians consists in the duration of the sinner's misery. And yet, while we are told that reason and conscience and natural affection, and our apprehension of the character of God, revolt against the belief in eternal punishment, we are to be satisfied with belief in ages of torment for the sinner, albeit the only possible explanation of hell, consistently with Divine love, is no longer applicable. If there be some necessity of which we know nothing, why fallen beings should continue to exist, then we can understand the Devil's presence in Eden and the fact of an eternal hell; but if the theories of conditional immortality be accepted, the continuance of evil in this world is no longer an intellectual difficulty only, but a moral difficulty of the gravest kind, and hell stands out as a hideous exhibition of wanton and remorseless wrath.

What then is the cost at which the theories of the annihilationist may be accepted as an article of the Christian faith? First, we must assume that death is extinction of being, which the Scripture unequivocally teaches it is not. Next, we must believe that God's first solemn warning against sin was an idle threat, which He had no intention of fulfilling; and that the truest word spoken to Adam was that which, for six thousand years, men have called "the Devil's lie," "Ye shall not surely die." More than this, we must recognise that the death of Christ was the destruction of His humanity, and His resurrection a piece of transcendental jugglery to conceal the Devil's triumph and deceive the saints of God, who for eighteen centuries have believed that the Blessed One Who wept at the grave of Lazarus, and sat travel-soiled and weary at Sychar's well, was upon the Father's throne as MAN, whereas His manhood perished upon Calvary, and He is no longer Man but only God. And all this mingled folly and error must be accepted, forsooth, to screen the reputation of Almighty God, now endangered by our belief in hell in the midst of nineteenth-century enlightenment!

---

1. Some of the Italian tyrants in the Middle Ages did this very thing; and a reverend opponent of eternal punishment has had the temerity to compare God to such a

monster, if there be an endless hell. If the author were not given up to a reprobate mind, he would have seen as he wrote the blasphemy that a thirty days' hell followed by extinction would more fully satisfy the analogy. His argument is against any hell whatever.
2. See *ante*.

CHAPTER 9
CONDITIONAL IMMORTALITY.

The ephemeral literature upon the subject of conditional immortality gives prominence to statements of a kind which, though generally excluded from standard works, have no little influence with ordinary minds. It is urged, for example, that the judgment upon sin was the death of the *soul*; and, it is added, the meaning of this can be realised by analogy, for just as the body is dissolved, and ceases to exist *as a body*, so shall it be with the *soul*. But this is to allow ourselves to be misled by using words in a loose and popular sense, unwarranted by Holy Writ. Scripture never speaks of the death of the soul. To quote in opposition to this the statement "The soul that sinneth, it shall die," is to trade upon the language of our English Bible. The word in the original means merely the person, the individual;

the father is not to suffer for the son, nor the son for the father, but the person who sins, *he* shall die.[1]

Neither does the Scripture speak of the death of the *body*. In our English version we read of "dead bodies," but not in the original. If our thought be of "natural death," the *body* comes into prominence; if of "spiritual death," the soul. But in either case it is *the man* who dies—not his body or his soul.[2]

It is urged again that just as a branch may continue to live for a time after it has been severed from the tree, so the sinner may exist for a time apart from God; but that when separated from Him Who is the fountain of life, he must, sooner or later, fade out of existence. Now, this of course is a mere theory, without the slightest pretence of proof. Moreover, it abandons the rival theory that sinners are miraculously preserved in existence with a view to punishment; and it assumes that their ultimate annihilation will be the result of natural law, and not of a Divine judgment. If this theory be true, there must, of course, be an average length of life for the soul as for the body. What the period is we cannot tell, but it must be more than six thousand years, for we know that all who have ever lived on earth shall continue in existence till the judgment. But when the judgment comes, the antediluvian dead will of course be comparatively near the end of their sorrow, in contrast with the lost of the latter days. The amount of punishment to be suffered by the sinner will thus depend, not on the guilt of his sin, but on the age of his soul at the time of the judgment. It is not strange that this view of the matter is ignored by writers of repute.

It would probably be found, however, that the large majority of those who refuse to believe in what they call "eternal evil" ignore all such arguments and theories as have been here discussed, They rest their convictions altogether on the indisputable fact that the Creator is able to put an end to the existence of His creatures. And such, they tell us, Scripture explicitly declares to be His purpose; for "Destruction," "Perdition," "The lake of fire," and other words of kindred import, plainly teach the annihilation of the ungodly. This belief deserves, and shall receive, the fullest consideration.

But let it be distinctly kept in view that this implies what is called the "natural immortality" of man. If by the law of his being he be destined to cease to exist, or if the death-penalty of sin imply extinction of being, the question here proposed cannot arise. They who raise it assume that but for the Divine interference in judgment man's existence would continue indefinitely; and they undertake to prove unequivocally from Scripture that the second death, unlike the first, will put an end to him altogether. According to them the element of the miraculous is not in the preservation of the sinner for the judgment, but in his annihilation in and by the judgment. They thus entirely abandon the position taken up by the leading advocates of conditional immortality, and there must be no attempt to fall back on that position, if Scripture, when appealed to, should refuse the testimony they claim from it. The single issue now remaining is whether the Bible teaches the extermination of the wicked; and the *onus* of proof rests entirely with those who maintain that it does. Man exists; and as no crisis or change of which we have any knowledge puts an end to that existence,[3] we must assume that it will continue indefinitely, unless the contrary be proved. But, we are assured, the Scriptures expressly teach that the wicked shall be put out of existence altogether. This is what has to be proved, and now we turn to examine the proofs.

That it is to the New Testament Scriptures we must look for a decision upon this question is a statement so obvious that most people will deem it superfluous. We are told, however, that "in the Hebrew tongue there are no less than fifty roots, meaning, habitually or occasionally, to destroy; most of which are used in the Old Testament to specify the ultimate doom of the wicked." A *dictum* of this kind is well fitted to overwhelm ordinary readers, who would never dream that an author of repute, writing on such solemn subjects, could make a statement wholly unfounded. But will the reader take up his Bible, and with the aid of a concordance seek out in the Hebrew Scriptures the more than fifty passages in which "the *ultimate doom* of the wicked" is "specified." His labours will lead to a startling result. Can he find ten such passages? Can he find FIVE? If his list should be a much longer one than is here anticipated, a glance at a Hebrew concordance will satisfy him that the same words which, as he supposes, describe eternal judgment, are elsewhere used of death, or of some other temporal judgment.[4] And he will find further that the extremely rare passages (such as Daniel xii. 2), which admittedly relate to the final state, are precisely those which the advocates of eternal punishment lay stress upon to prove their doctrine.

Daniel's prophecy above referred to is the *only* passage in the Old Testament which plainly announces the resurrection of the wicked. And when in the Epistle of Jude the inspired writer seeks a prophecy of the great judgment to come, he finds it in the words of Enoch, outside the canon altogether. Account for it as we may, the silence of the Old Testament Scriptures as to the final state is one of the most striking features of the revelation. It is not merely "life and immortality" which have been brought to light by the gospel; it is there also that the dark alternative has been plainly revealed. But even those who would reject the position here assumed as regards the scope of the Old Testament, would freely admit that the ultimate appeal must be to the New.

An admission which fairness demands may somewhat clear the ground. The language of the New Testament describing the destruction of the lost is perfectly consistent with the doctrine of conditional immortality. And further, this is all that needs to be proved by authors such as those that have here been quoted, assuming always the validity and success of the arguments on which their position rests. But that is not the question here. These arguments have been examined, and they have been found, not only fallacious, but destructive of "the faith once delivered." The question now is, whether those who reject these reasonings can apart from them altogether find proof in the Scripture that the doom of the wicked is annihilation.

With some, this question will resolve itself into an inquiry whether the word *destruction* correctly expresses the Greek original in the passages where it is used. But this will not bear investigation. Extinction or annihilation is not necessarily implied in the word at all. So far from this being its primary meaning, it is a very remote signification. In the classical use of the word, to *destroy* a thing is to do it irreparable injury, to unfit it permanently for the purpose for which it was intended. Its meaning as used of a *person* may be illustrated by a quotation which ought to be familiar to all who speak the

English tongue—"No freeman shall be taken or imprisoned, or be disseised of his freehold or liberties or free customs, or be outlawed or exiled or any otherwise *destroyed*, but by lawful judgment of his peers or by the law of the land." According to Magna Charta, then, to drive a man from his home, to deprive him of his property, or to shut him up in prison, is to *destroy* him.[5] The thought that we would convey by ruin our ancestors expressed by destroy. The word, therefore, may be fitly used to describe the doom of the wicked, whatever that doom may be. But the meaning of a word depends upon the use of it. Judged by this test, what is the force of the expression in the New Testament?

There are ten words rendered *destroy* in the Authorised Version, and three of these occur also in the substantive form as *destruction*. A full list of these words will be found in the Appendix; but there are only three of them which need be noticed here, as these alone are used to describe the final state of the lost.

We read in 2 Thessalonians ii. 8, that at His coming the Lord shall *destroy* the Lawless One, the Antichrist. The word here used (*katargeo*) occurs again in Hebrews ii. 14 of the destruction of the Devil at and by the death of Christ. It means to render powerless, or useless, or inoperative (Rom iii. 3, 31, *ex. gr.*), and hence "to do away," or "destroy," in the Magna Charta sense. The same word is used of death in i Corinthians xv. 26 and 2 Timothy 3 10. For the believer, death was "destroyed" de *jure* at the cross, and will be "abolished" *de facto* in the glory. The thought of annihilation cannot be imported into this word at all.

The next word, a very much stronger term for "destruction," is used for "natural death" in the only passage where it occurs as a verb. Four times only it is used as a noun (*olethros*), and in each of these the word ruin would exactly convey the thought intended. In 1 Corinthians v. 5, a certain person is delivered to Satan "for the destruction of the flesh," albeit we find in 2 Corinthians ii. 6 that this same person, having profited by his "punishment," was restored to the fellowship of the Church. In i Thessalonians v. 3 we are told that at the advent of Christ "sudden *destruction*" shall come upon the ungodly. Is this annihilation? By no means, for, as Scripture elsewhere will tell us, they shall be "reserved to the day of judgment to be punished." The same remark applies to the statement in 2 Thessalonians i. 9. And, moreover, it is "everlasting destruction *from the face* of the Lord": it is banishment and not annihilation which characterises the ruin. In the last remaining passage where this word occurs, St. Paul declares that the lusts begotten of money-worship "drown men in *destruction* and perdition." Is this annihilation? And yet the Greek language contains no stronger terms to express the idea.[6]

The word rendered "perdition" in the verse just

quoted is the last which claims mention here. It is perhaps the most important of all. The noun (*apōleia*) occurs twenty times, the verb (*appollumi*) ninety-two times, in the New Testament. A reference to the Concordance will show that it is sometimes used as a synonym for *death* in the ordinary sense, and in several passages it describes the *present* state of the impenitent. Christ came "to save that which was *lost*." In the parables, the sheep was lost, the piece of silver was *lost*, the prodigal son was *lost*. So in every passage where the subject or the context enables us to fix the meaning with certainty, the word means a condition of existence, not a ceasing to exist.[7]

He who gives a cup of cold water to a disciple "shall in no wise lose his reward." Christ was "not sent but unto the lost sheep of the House of Israel." If a man put new wine into old bottles "the bottles will be *marred*."

"The thief cometh not, but for to steal, and to kill, and to *destroy*." In the Appendix will be found a list including every passage where this word occurs, and the reader can judge for himself whether in its use in Scripture it means annihilation. And let it not be forgotten that if the words here noticed fail to convey that idea, the Greek language has none other to express it.[8]

But the lake of fire—is not that annihilation? How can any creature live in the midst of fire? The question need not be discussed; neither need we consider whether *fire* be here a figure, as elsewhere in Scripture, to express fierce trouble and judgment. These are speculative inquiries. The practical question which concerns us is settled beyond dispute by the plain testimony of Scripture. In the judgment scene of the 25th chapter of Matthew the "eternal fire" is expressly called "eternal punishment"; and though the word rendered "punishment" be denied its classical meaning of corrective discipline, it cannot possibly signify annihilation.[9]

The Lord's words in the narrative of Lazarus and Dives are plainer still. The sinner is there represented as in a condition of conscious and active existence in hell.[10] And still more definite is the language of the very Scripture where the lake of fire is mentioned.[11] The Devil is to be cast into the lake of fire. This, therefore, must be the "fire prepared for the Devil," spoken of in Matthew xxv. 41. And it is declared that the Devil, the beast, and the false prophet shall be there "tormented for ever and ever." If such language can be construed to signify sudden annihilation, words may mean anything. This, moreover, is what Scripture declares will be "the second death."

---

1. See tho use of the same word in Lev. v. 2, 4, 15 : "If a soul touch," etc., "If a soul swear," etc., "If a soul commit a trespass." In Lev. vii. 20 we have "The soul that eateth;" and in xxi. 11 it is translated "body."

2. James ii. 26 is the only seeming exception to the above statement. But the context shows that there the word *dead* is used in the same secondary or figurative sense as when we speak of a stone or a log being dead. And no English writer would use our word kill as it is used in Matt. X. 28. According to Liddell and Scott it means, first, to kill, slay; secondly, to condemn to death; thirdly, to weary to death, to torment.
3. Here I am dealing only with those who accept revelation.
4. Any one who has access to a good library will find in the "Englishman's Hebrew Concordance" all the materials necessary to enable him to settle this question for himself.
5. It is an interesting fact that among the peasantry of the west and south of Ireland, with whom English is an acquired language, this is the common meaning of *destroy*. Any one who is evicted, or robbed, or ill-treated, is said to be "destroyed."
6. The champion of Conditional Immortality remarks on I Tim. vi. 9: "As the Greek language does not afford two stronger expressions than these for denoting the idea of literal death and extinction of being, it requires a large amount of evidence to prove that they were intended by St. Paul to convey the idea of indestructible existence in torment." No one whose mind was not thoroughly warped by dwelling on this controversy would imagine for a moment that the Apostle here intended to convey *either* "extinction of being" *or* "indestructible existence in torment."

    But the admission above made is valuable. These are the strongest expressions possible to express annihilation. That the first does not express that thought is certain, for if it did the addition of the second would be mere verbiage.
7. Matt. x. 28 demands special notice on account of the use which has been made of it: "Fear not them which kill the body, but are not able to kill the soul; but rather fear Him which is able to destroy both soul and body in hell." Assume that "death" and "destruction" imply extinction, and this settles the whole question. But if, refusing to as-

sume anything of the sort, we analyse the words here used and consider what they were intended to convey, the thought we shall take in is this: man's power can reach the body only, not the soul; but God can destroy both. If we want to know what "destroy" means, we must inquire how the Lord used the word elsewhere, and this is precisely what I am now investigating.

8. Of the Antichrist it is written, "whom the Lord shall *consume* with the spirit of His mouth" (2 Thess. ii. 8). The meaning of the word may be gathered from the only other passage where St. Paul uses it: "If ye bite and devour one another take heed that ye be not *consumed* one of another" (Gal. V. 15).

   Devour, in Heb. x. 27, is the common word for *eating*, here used in a figurative sense. In I Peter v. 8, a like use is made of the word generally rendered *to swallow*.

9. Matt. XXV. 41 and 46. The kindred verb occurs Acts iv. 2 1 and 2 Peter ii. 9, only. It means primarily to prune (trees), to curtail, or check; and then to chastise or punish. Dr. Trench (*Synonyms*) denies to it in Scripture the special sense it bears in classical Greek of *corrective* punishment.

10. Luke xvi. 19-31. Some perhaps may object that his is not the final state of the lost; but this question need not be discussed, for the sinner is in the flames of Gehenna (*cf.* vers. 23, 24), and therefore the fire, whatever it means, does not imply extinction. I really must decline to notice the view of the passage urged by one of the writers cited in an earlier chapter, which represents Dives as "one of the elect people."

11. Rev. xix. 20, xx. 10, 14, 15, xxi. i.

CHAPTER 10
THE QUESTION RESTATED.

The results recorded in preceding chapters are doubtless a surprise. What then is to be the general conclusion? It was a revolt against the dogmas of certain schools of theology which led to this inquiry : Must we at last fall back on the very position we thus abandoned? Must we be content, after all, to accept the horrors of mediaeval eschatology, which try the faith of Christians, and not only deepen but embitter the unbelief of sceptics? Before resigning ourselves to this as a last alternative, surely it behoves us to turn back once more to Scripture, and with care and earnestness and patience to inquire how far the difficulties which here perplex us may depend upon the ignorance of finite minds; how far upon excrescences, the growth of human teaching, by which the truth has been distorted or concealed.

What are these difficulties? That God should tolerate the existence of evil for eternity. That the brief life-sin of finite creatures should lead to punishment of infinite duration. That no matter how dense and hopeless the darkness in which that life is spent, their destiny should be fixed irreversibly at death. That the overwhelming majority of the human race are doomed to exist for ever in a scene of unutterable horror. That while Christ shall have His thousands, the Devil shall boast of millions in his train. That these, the creatures of a God of love, shall be abandoned to the outer darkness, the gnashing of teeth, the torment day and night for ever and ever. That banished from love and light and peace to their awful prison home, Satan shall reign over them for evermore, and his foul demons shall revel in their anguish. And that this shall be for all without distinction. That the myriad millions of the heathen who never heard of the God of Heaven shall know Him first and only and for ever as the God of *Hell*. That the good and pure of earth, and little children too, in countless hosts, whose life was quenched ere ever they had fairly launched upon the sea of sin, shall be herded with the vilest and the worst of men and trampled on by devils; in time to grow like them, until at last all trace and memory of purity and good shall perish, and hell itself shall lose its power to make the damned more hateful, more corrupt, so hideous and awful shall be the depths of their depravity and guilt.

And that this shall be for ever, FOR EVER. That no moving shadow on the dial shall relieve despair by reminding the lost that every day of anguish brings them nearer to deliverance. Just as the tree is said to put forth its roots in exact proportion to its spreading branches, so we could understand if punishment in the under-world were measured by each sinner's life on earth. This would silence unbelief; all would freely own its equity. But that the doom of the lost shall be *eternal* punishment, this is a conception which paralyses human thought. With the great majority of Christians it is the chief, if not the only, difficulty.

As already stated, a single wave of human life comprises over fourteen hundred millions of mankind. But none will dream that even one of these shall be forgotten. When the judgment comes, it will not be only the great of earth who shall stand before the throne. "The dead, *small and great*" shall be there. God's great judgments in this world were awful in the suddenness with which all without distinction were engulfed in a common doom. The hoary sinner and the helpless infant perished together under the waters of the Flood. So was it again when fire from heaven consumed the Cities of the Plain. But this was just because there is a judgment to come, and another world beyond, in which perfect justice can be meted out to each. The glimpses afforded us behind the veil which hides that judgment and that world are few and partial; but this much is absolutely certain, that the lost will not be sent to their doom unheard. Twice in Scripture they are represented as parleying with their Judge.[1] Each one shall be fairly dealt with. The record of each life shall be laid bare. The books shall be opened, and the dead shall be judged, every man according to his works.[2] Every sinner in the countless multitude to be arraigned at the great assize shall hear his indictment, and be heard in his defence. How long then shall be allowed to each? Take the estimated population of the world for this one century in which we live: suppose that for this purpose every human being is allotted less than a quarter of an hour—a brief quarter of an hour; assume that the session shall go on unceasingly, without a moment's interval, hour after hour, day after day, year after year, till all has been concluded; and the judgment of this small section of the human race will last *one hundred thousand years*! And were we to estimate the number of those who have lived and died during the sixty centuries already past, and of those who are still to be born upon the earth, we should be forced to the conclusion that the duration of the "day of judgment" shall be measured *by millions of years!*

Need a single word be added to emphasise the folly of measuring the events of that world by the calendars of time? That some fallacy underlies the problem the very statement of it proves; but wherein that fallacy consists we cannot tell. If human reason were under obligations to solve the enigma, the solution might possibly be found in the theories of Kant. In the whole range of metaphysical inquiry no more philosophical suggestion was ever offered than his, that Time is nothing more than a law of human thought. And though neither he nor any of his disciples ever dreamt of his system being turned to such account, may it not be used as the basis of an appeal to Christians to trust God for the explanation of a difficulty which is purely intellectual?[3]

To lay stress, therefore, upon *eternal* evil is merely to conceal the real question which, if faith is to depend on the absence of difficulties, reason is bound to give some account of. If the theories of geologists be well founded, this earth must have been the grave of an earlier creation before it became the cradle and home of existing life. And if there was death, there must also have been sin. Some have conjectured that Satan was the federal head of that earlier creation, and that his peculiar enmity to man was because this earth had once been his own domain. At all events the fact is clear that sin and death had been active in the universe of God before the Adamic age. Whether the interval since Satan's fall had been a century or a million years, the moral difficulty is just the same.

Though infinite in power and goodness, God permitted a fallen being to exist, albeit the result was the ruin of Adam and his world. What possible explanation can be offered of this fact, if "the extermination of evil◊" be His plan and purpose? It is the *existence* of evil which is the real difficulty. To accept the fact of Satan's existence during all the ages of our world, and to hold it incredible that he should continue to exist when his power for evil shall have ceased for ever—this is neither faith nor philosophy, but an *ad captandum* appeal to human ignorance and to the awe inspired in finite minds by the attempt to realise eternity.

This last remark suggests another point in the popular travesty of truth respecting the final condition of the lost. The "everlasting fire" is not to be the Devil's kingdom. It will be his prison, not his palace. Amidst so much that is doubtful, this at least is sure. "At the name of Jesus *every* knee shall bow," in heaven, earth, and hell; every tongue shall own Him Lord.[4] "*All things* shall be subdued unto Him."[5] Not until "He shall have put down all rule and all authority and power" will He deliver up the kingdom to the Father.[6] Every creature in the universe shall be in absolute subjection to Almighty God. The underworld is not to be a scene of Satanic carnival. The word-pictures which describe the shrieks and curses of the lost of earth, as demons mock their anguish or heap fuel on their torture fires, are relieved from the charge of folly only by the graver charge of profanity. There is no spot in all the Queen's dominions in which the reign of order is so supreme as in a prison. So shall it be in hell.

To speak of this as producing an alleviation of the sinner's doom betrays the lingering influence of the error here condemned. Obedience will be their normal condition there. To speculate how it will be brought about is idle. It may be that the recognition of the perfect justice and goodness of God will lead the lost to accept their doom. Possibly, too, the poet's dream may yet be realised, that Divine love shall shine out so clearly, even amid the fires of judgment, that when the anthem rises in the palace-home of God, even the prison-house shall join in the refrain, and praise shall issue forth from hell. Speculations such as these are perfectly legitimate in poetry, but they should have no place in the sober prose of theology.

To plead that God will still own the bond which binds His creatures to Himself is to forget that the great revelation of GRACE implies that all relationships were broken, all claims lost, by the murder of the Son. To argue that "the resurrection of judgment is one part of the redeeming work of Christ," and that "the judgment of the lost is based on a present work of the Redeemer," is to confound redemption itself with the place and power which Christ has taken in connection with redemption. It was not the Cross which made Him either Son of

God or Son of Man, albeit it was in view of our redemption that He was thus revealed. Yet it is as Son of God that He shall recall the dead to life. And it is "because He is the Son of Man" that all judgment is committed to Him.[7]

In considering the destiny of mankind, it is of immense importance to vindicate the Bible from the reproach which mediaeval theology has brought on it. But if the statements of Scripture must needs be coloured or explained away by theories which eliminate all element of dread from the doom of the impenitent, *faith* is of course impossible. If the reader will pursue the inquiry to the close, he will find that those statements, unspeakably solemn and awful though they be, present no difficulty which a reverent and believing heart will refuse to leave with a God Whose justice and goodness and love are beyond all question and all doubt.

---

1. Matt. xxv. 44; Luke xiii. 25, 26.
2. Rev. xx. 12, 13.
3. I wish to guard against misrepresentation here. I appeal to the Transcendental philosophy, not as affording the true solution of the difficulty—nothing is farther from my thought—but as a protest against allowing faith to waver in presence of a difficulty which can be so easily disposed of.
4. Phil. ii. 10, 11.
5. I Cor. xv. 28.
6. Ib, ver. 24.

7. John V. 25- 27. The writer specially referred to in the above paragraph seeks to establish his point by assuming that Scripture statements on this subject are marked by a contradiction ("antithesis," he calls it), to be accounted for by the creature being viewed sometimes in a personal, sometimes in a federal aspect. Such a theory is always open to suspicion : here it seems wholly baseless. The passages he cites to illustrate it are I Cor. xv. 22, as compared with Rom. ii. 7; and Gal. vi. 2, 5. If the exposition of I Cor. xv. offered at p. 183 *post*, be accepted, that passage may not be used as he suggests. And the seeming contradiction in Gal. vi. 2, 5, depends on the poverty of our translation. *Burden* in that passage represents two words in the original. βάρος denotes the pressure of a weight which may be transferred; φορτίον the load which each must carry for himself. In this world every one has his own proper load to bear; but some are *burdened*, and to relieve such is to fulfil the law of Christ.

CHAPTER II
THE QUESTION DISCUSSED.

The record of the Augustinian doctrine of the damnation of infants is one of the darkest chapters in theology.[1] If we distinguish between what is doubtful and what is doubted, the question is not open to discussion. No language can be plainer than that in which the Epistle to the Romans teaches that Christ's redemption is as far-reaching in its effects as Adam's sin.

It is not that all shall be saved through the death of Christ, but that, in virtue of that death, no one shall be lost save by reason of personal guilt.[2] It is certain, therefore, that the infant dead, whether of heathen or of Christian lands, shall be reckoned among the number of the redeemed.

And where does Scripture teach that those who live and die in heathen darkness shall not hear of

Christ after they pass away from earth? Either to assert or to deny that such shall find a "place of repentance" in the underworld is the arrogance which springs from ignorance; and in this sphere all arrogance is profane. It may be urged that if the sinners of the days of Noah have since received a gospel message from the Lord Himself,[3] all others who have been denied a revelation upon earth shall have mercy offered them beyond. On the other hand, it may be argued that as "the exception proves the rule," so the special mention of the sinners who perished in the Flood implies that their case was peculiar, if not unique. The fact is, the Bible was not written to gratify curiosity in matters which in no way concern us. As regards the destiny of those it fails to reach, it is absolutely silent. The fate of the heathen is with God.[4]

There is one passage, indeed, which unfolds with definiteness the principles of judgment applicable to all mankind. The reference, of course, is to the second chapter of the Epistle to the Romans, and the apostle's statements are of such importance here that it may be well to quote them fully. He speaks of "the righteous judgment of God, Who will render to every one according to his deeds : to them who by patient continuance in well-doing, seek for glory and honour and immortality, eternal life; but to them that are contentious, and do not obey the truth, but obey unrighteousness, indignation and wrath, tribulation and anguish upon every soul of man that doeth evil, of the Jew first and also of the Gentile; but glory, honour, and peace to every one that worketh good, to the Jew first and also to the Gentile. For there is no respect of persons with God. For as many as have sinned without law shall also perish without law, and as many as have sinned under law shall be judged by law, in the day when God shall judge the secrets of men by Jesus Christ."

Here are principles of universal application : who will deny their equity? Many seem to think that salvation by faith sets all this aside; but such thoughts are wholly false. When appealed to by the people to give some clear light to guide them in the life of well-doing, the Lord's answer was explicit, *"This is the work of God*, that ye believe on Him Whom He hath sent."[5] The standard of well-doing was changed by His advent, but the principle was the same. Allegiance to a banished prince may show itself in many ways; but once he appears within the realm, personal homage becomes the test and touchstone of loyalty. So is it as between God and men. Some live in nature's darkness: some in the blaze of gospel light. But whether it be merely "the candle set up within them," or the full revelation of the Son of God, "to obey the truth" is to tread the path of blessing. The heathen will not be damned for ignorance of Christ; while, on the other hand, in Christendom no amount of seeming "well-doing" will avail, if personal loyalty to Christ be wanting. The word spoken retrospectively of His life on earth shall still hold good when He returns to judgment: "To as many as *received Him*, to them gave He the right to become children of God."[6]

But, it will be answered, this is evading the real issue, which is as to the equity, not of the judgment, but of the sentence. If everlasting torment be the penalty of sin, such must be in fact the doom of the vast majority of the heathen. It is idle to theorise upon the supposed statistics of the Day of Judgment, though the popular belief is largely based upon wilful and deliberate rejection of Scripture testimony about coming ages of blessing upon earth.[7] But where does Scripture teach that everlasting torment is the penalty of *sin*? DEATH is the penalty of sin. Instead of absolute equality, Scripture indicates an infinite inequality in punishment.

There will be the "few stripes" and the "many stripes." God "will render to each *according to his deeds*." Surely the distinction is obvious and simple between the general penalty of sin, which depends on the essential character of a God Who cannot tolerate evil in His presence, and the special kind and measure of punishment which the Righteous Judge will impose on each, according to the degree and nature of his guilt. It is of the Antichrist and his adherents—the enemies of Christ in the awful days to come—that the Word declares they "shall be tormented day and night for ever and ever."[8]

And this disposes of a difficulty which has been used with such success in the interests of error. Sin's penalty has indeed been borne by Christ. His resurrection was the public proof that every claim of righteousness was satisfied and all who by faith become identified with Him are justified from sin. But the sufferings of the Sin-bearer did not include the consequences of rejecting the atonement. When, therefore, it is demanded whether Christ endured "everlasting torment," the best reply is to expose the latent error in the question. To speak even of His bearing the *punishment* of sin is to use unscriptural language; and the statement is untrue, if punishment be intended to embrace all the consequences, both providential and penal, which follow upon transgression.

The attempt to eliminate all element of mystery from the atonement is impious and vain. Redemption is, in fact, the crowning mystery of revelation. But it is mainly in the imputation of sin that the mystery consists. It is not, as so often stated, "the innocent dying for the guilty," for that would be immoral, and impossible with God; but the innocent passing into the place of the guilty, and, as *guilty*, dying to expiate the guilt imputed to Him. If any one still insists upon the inquiry, How could sin be so imputed to the sinless as to make a vicarious death justifiable? he may seek to reason out the answer; but, as Bishop Butler says, "All conjectures about it must be, if not evidently absurd, yet at least uncertain." "Nor," he adds, "has any one reason to complain for want of further information, unless he can show his claim to it."[9] The fact is plain—and this alone concerns us—that "He Who knew no sin *was made sin* for us."

"During all His ministry on earth, albeit it was spent in humiliation and reproach, no hand was ever laid upon the Blessed One, save in importunate supplication or in devout and loving service. But when at times His enemies would fain have seized Him, a mysterious hour to come was spoken of, in which their hate should be unhindered. 'This is your hour, and the power of darkness,' He exclaimed, as Judas and the impious companions in his guilt drew round Him in the garden. *His* hour He called it when He thought of His mission upon earth; their hour, when, in the fulfilment of that mission, He found Himself within their grasp.

"The agonies inflicted on Him by men have taken hold on the mind of Christendom; but beyond and above all these the mystery of the Passion is that He was forsaken and accursed of God. In some sense, indeed, His sufferings from men were but a consequence of this; therefore His reply to Pilate, 'Thou couldest have no power at all against Me, except it were given thee from above.' If men seized and slew Him it was because God had delivered Him up. When that destined hour had struck, the mighty hand drew back which till then had shielded Him from outrage. His death was not the beginning, but the close of His sufferings; in truth, it was the hour of His triumph."[10]

To be "forsaken and accursed of God"—this is death in its deeper spiritual significance. And the fact is clear, however it be explained, that once the Lord had passed into that condition, the only way of escape from it was by laying down His life. If the penalty of sin be "natural death" merely, the agony of Gethsemane and "Immanuel's orphan cry" upon the cross can in no way be accounted for. If it be annihilation, then the death of Christ was a defeat and not a triumph, and, as already shown, His resurrection was a fraud. Faith grasps the fact that the death of the Sin-bearer, in all which it implies, is an equivalent to the sinner's doom, but how it is so is a mystery which reason seeks in vain to solve.

Experience teaches us that even in this world the consequences of sin are disastrous and abiding. And Scripture leaves no doubt that in the world to come sin's punishment shall be real and searching. We know that it will entail banishment from God; and further we know that infinite love and perfect justice shall measure the cup which each must drink. But beyond this we know absolutely nothing. The pride of intellect which lured our first parents to their ruin is abnormally developed in their posterity; but man's vain boast of knowledge beyond what is revealed serves only to awaken echoes which proclaim his folly.

What concerns us is not to theorise about the penalty of *sin*, but to take heed that we escape the "sorer punishment" of despising grace. It were otherwise if Christianity gave those who reject it the alternative of falling back on the position held by all whom the revelation has never reached. But no such choice is ours. The Gospel shuts men up either to accept the blessings it bestows, or else to await the doom of which those shall be "thought worthy" who have "trodden under foot the Son of God."[11] To cease to exist is to become as though one had not been; but a fate worse than this awaits the Christ-rejector and the apostate—"Good were it for that man, if he had never been born."

---

1. The more one studies the Fathers the wider appears to be the gulf which separates their writings from the inspired Scriptures. This remark applies with full force to Origen, whose writings are appealed to so confidently in this controversy.
2. On Rom. v. see App.
3. I Peter iii. 19, 20. I am here assuming that such is the meaning of the passage, although I own to having serious doubts upon the point. As Dean Alford says, the literature of the passage is almost a library in itself. His own note is an admirable summary of that library. Dean Plumptre's book is somewhat disappointing on this particular passage, from which it derives its name.
4. Passages such as Psalm ix. 15 - 20, which may seem an exception, do not speak of the *final* state at all, but only of God's providential judgments. The "hell" of the passage is

hades. "The wicked shall be turned into *sheol*, and all the nations that forget God.

5. John vi. 28, 29.
6. John i. 12.
7. The Bible is full of promises and prophecies of a time to come when God shall be known and feared from pole to pole. For aught we know, the population of the world will then be ten, or perchance a hundred times greater than at present. If we take this into account, together with the facts and possibilities of redemption noticed m the last few pages, is it so clear on which side the majority of mankind shall ultimately be found? It may be said that this is an appeal to our ignorance. True, but the prejudice I seek thus to break down is based entirely on our ignorance. The one is a set-off against the other : faith will ignore both, and leave the issue with God.
8. Rev. xiv. 11, xx. 10. On the word "torment," see App.
9. *The Analogy*, part ii., ch. v., § 6.
10. *The Coming Prince* (2nd ed.) pp. 1 16-17. The passage proceeds: "The midnight agony in Gethsemane was thus the great antitype of that midnight scene in Egypt, when the destroying angel flashed through the land. And as His death was the fulfilment of His people's deliverance, so it took place upon the anniversary of 'that self-same day that the Lord did bring the children of Israel out of Egypt by their armies.'" And attention is also called to the fact that the crucifixion was likewise the anniversary of the promise to Abraham. So the resurrection was the anniversary of the crossing of the Red Sea, and also of the resting of the ark on Mount Ararat.
11. Heb. x. 29.

CHAPTER 12
THE QUESTION ANSWERED.

To the reverent and refined there is something far more awful in the solemn measured language of Holy Writ upon the doom of the lost, than in all the word-pictures framed on it by facile pens or fluent tongues. These serve rather to repel, sometimes even to disgust. The outer darkness, the worm that never dies, the fire that is not quenched, the torment of the burning lake—all this may be but figurative language; but if so, the figures must represent realities still more terrible. It is easy to create a prejudice against the truth by giving prominence to human utterances, often foolish, sometimes coarse and profane, while studiously keeping out of view the great truth—love to a lost world. But it is the same gospel which reveals that love which also declares the coming wrath.[1] Just in proportion, therefore, as redemption is depreciated, the guilt of rejecting mercy will be ignored.

Man claims to be the arbiter of his own destiny, and "reason and conscience" tell him that "finite sin" shall have a finite punishment. But who will dare to call it "finite sin" to kill the Prince of Life? And such is the guilt of sinners who reject Him—"they crucify to themselves the Son of God, and put Him to an open shame."[2] To strike a fellow-man might be an offence, though possibly a trivial one. To strike a parent would be, morally at least, a heinous crime. But to strike a king would be treason, punishable with death. In every case the guilt and penalty are measured, not by the act itself, but by the position of the outraged person and his relationship to the offender. So is it as between God and men. "Half measures are impossible in view of the cross of Christ. The day is past when God could plead with men about their *sins*. The controversy now is not about a broken law, but a rejected Christ. If judgment, therefore, be our portion, it must be measured by God's estimate of the murder of His Son."[3]

But who are they who shall be held guilty of this direst sin? The answer is with God, and not with us. If any who have heard the gospel can prove that they are guiltless, we may be assured that "the Righteous Judge" will accept the plea. But let no one dare to trade upon a hope of mercy in that day, while putting mercy from him here and now. Men speak as though the gospel were nothing but a dogma which some may fairly doubt, and the many fail to understand, forgetting that the death of Christ is a great public fact which must bring either blessing or judgment to every soul to whom the testimony comes. The question is not of assent to a shibboleth, but of loyalty to a person; not of belief in salvation, but of devotion to a Saviour. But all this is lost in the religious scepticism of the day, which is eating the very heart out of Christianity.

> *"The Christ of ages past*
> *Is now the Christ no more;*
> *Altar and fire are gone,*
> *The Victim but a dream!"*

Hence the deep and widespread conspiracy that exists to make light both of the guilt and the punishment of sin. Self and not God having become the test and touch-stone of all things, sin is palliated and judgment decried. Men speak as though the love of God were on its trial at the bar of "reason and conscience," and as if the verdict must needs be deferred till the sinner's doom shall have been declared. But the love of God has been once and for ever vindicated by the great sacrifice of Calvary. It is measured by the gift of Christ, not by the lightness of their doom who reject Him. "*In this* was manifested the love of God toward us, because that God sent His only begotten Son into the world that we might live through Him."[4] "God *so loved* the world that He gave His only begotten Son, that whosoever believeth in Him should not perish, but have everlasting life."[5]

Here we have reached what is at once the real centre of the controversy and the climax of the argument. The preceding pages are the reflex of the struggle by which one inquirer has escaped from the difficulties set forth in the opening chapter. Perchance the record may prove helpful to others. The destiny of the lost is a great mystery, but it is only one phase of the crowning mystery of Evil. There must be some moral necessity why evil once existing, should continue to exist. Otherwise, the presence of the Serpent in Eden, and all the dismal facts of human history, would be inexplicable. But if the existence of Evil be recognised, its punishment is, in the very nature of things, inevitable. The real question, therefore, is not primarily as to the kind and duration of the punishment, but whether Divine love and equity have been placed beyond the shadow of a doubt. And that question will be answered by each according to his estimate of the gospel.

There is no question as to the Creator's power to extinguish creature existence; and by redemption God has won the undoubted right to restore the fallen race to blessing. But who can tell what moral hindrances may govern the exercise of that power and that right? Scripture assumes the continued existence of the Adam life. The resurrection is a proof of it. Judgment and hell are themselves an overwhelming proof of it. The crowning proof of it is redemption achieved at a cost so priceless. But if the scepticism of the day could be forced to speak out plainly, it would declare that God is to blame for human sin, and therefore redemption is merely the natural outcome of Divine benevolence. Any good man who, through his own default, allowed ruin to overtake others dependent on him, would make any sacrifice to repair the evil. Is man, then, better than God? Will not God make further and unceasing efforts to restore the lost whom love and grace shall have failed to win? Or, if that be impossible, will He not in mercy put an end to their existence?

The only answer to all such cavils is the cross of Christ. Behind that cross there is no concealed reserve of mercy or love. Man has lost through sin the paradise of earth; God bids him welcome to the paradise of heaven. The sin was in spite of all that God had done for man. The blessing is in spite of all the return that man has made to God. Men plead that because of what they are they cannot be what they ought to be; but redemption is for those who are all they ought not to be. Grace is as free as sunlight. God "will have all men to be saved and to come to the knowledge of the truth." It is "for the Devil and his angels" that the "everlasting fire" is prepared; God's own heaven is thrown open to the lost of earth. The weakest or the worst of men has but to choose Christ, and not sin, and he will find in Christ a Saviour from sin, and attain to blessing such as unfallen Adam never dreamed of. But what if he choose sin and reject Christ? God declares that the alternative to grace is wrath; but the religious scepticism of the day will tell him that he may despise grace and yet escape wrath; or, at all events, that the wrath will be tempered and limited according to his own estimate of his guilt.

The possession of a single share in a commercial company is regarded by an English judge as a sufficient reason for leaving the bench if that company be sued; and yet, in rehearsing the Day of Judgment, men claim to sit as assessors with Almighty God, and to adjudicate upon their own destiny.

We conclude, then, that the proclamation of grace in the gospel is final, and that the destiny of all who either receive or reject the message is fixed in this life. In the Lord's own words, "He that believeth on Him is not condemned; but he that believeth not is already condemned."[6] At death, therefore, the unbeliever passes hence to await, not his trial, but his sentence. Further, we conclude that in the case of all mankind the judgment of the great day will be irreversible. But whether those who have been denied a revelation in this world shall find "a place of repentance" in the intermediate state, it is not for us to dogmatise.

To deny that God can give blessing to those whom the voice of revelation has never reached, is to make the value of redemption depend on man's appreciation of it. To assert that the testimony shall be granted to all mankind is to ignore the apostle's statement that "as many as have sinned without law shall also perish without law." What the fate of such will be we cannot tell. That they will reap what they have sown, the Scripture plainly states.[7] And this suggests that in one aspect of it, "future punishment may follow wickedness in the way of natural consequence."[8] Death is the *wages* of sin. But if there were nothing more in future punishment than this, then, as already urged, there would be no need whatever of a day of judgment. Once we pass beyond the general statements of Scripture, we know absolutely nothing of the fate of the lost.

Of course, we can launch out in speculations. There are no idlers in a well-disciplined gaol: in God's great prison-house is idleness to reign supreme? The tread-mill, which in former times served only to grind the air, is in our day used for good and needful purposes: are we to suppose that all the energies of the lost are to be consumed in tasks of aimless punishment? God has told us of their punishment, for that is all we are concerned to know; but nowhere has He said that it is for punishment alone they shall exist. If throughout creation, and even in the world which the microscope reveals to us, every creature seems to have its mission, why should we assume it will be otherwise in hell? It were but folly to press the matter further, and theorise about the possible employments of the lost; but may we not suppose that in the infinite wisdom of God there are purposes to the accomplishment of which even they will be made to minister? If heaven were the fools' paradise of our hymnology, the conventional hell might well be accepted as its counterpart. If the redeemed are to sit in one vast surpliced choir, to spend eternity in song, why should not the lost be battened down in some huge dungeon, with no occupation save to bewail for evermore their doom?

One of the commonest artifices in this controversy is to seize on the popular conception of hell, and then to demand whether existence in such a condition for millions of ages be not incredible. Let any one put his heaven to the same test, and he will be startled at reaching a like conclusion. That an eternal paradise will be eternal happiness the believer is assured. But it is entirely a matter of faith. Reason cannot grasp it. The mind is utterly overwhelmed by the attempt to realise eternity at all.

On this whole subject "orthodoxy" has gone beyond what Scripture warrants, and "heresy" ignores or denies some of its plainest teaching. Our choice, however, does not lie between orthodoxy and heresy, as judged by creeds and Churches, but between revelation on the one hand, and the opinions of men on the other. In a sphere where reason can tell us nothing, we are bound to keep strictly to the very words of Scripture, neither enlarging their scope nor drawing inferences from them. But in contrast with this, the inspired words have been used in such a way as to produce a mental revolt which endangers faith. Divine love is boundless. Christ's redemption is of infinite value. Grace is supreme; and it is "salvation-bringing to all men" —such is its scope and tendency. But even if it were certain that in the underworld God will reveal Himself as a Saviour to those who fail to hear of Him thus on earth, this would only emphasize the truth which is as plain on the page of Scripture as words can make it, that the gospel of His grace is a *final* revelation to those it reaches.

Man boasts of the proud but perilous dignity of an independent will. He used it in turning away from God. He may use it again in refusing to turn back to God. And what then? The gospel of a free pardon through the death of Christ is "preached in the whole creation under heaven." The amnesty has been proclaimed; and, because God is unwilling that any should perish, judgment waits. But if men despise the grace and reject the Saviour, the sure and inevitable alternative is PERDITION.

Strange it is that they who are most emphatic in asserting that God must give salvation to *all* men in the next world, are precisely those who dismiss as fanaticism the truth that He gives salvation here and now to those who seek Him.

The Church of Rome denies grace altogether, and represents Divine love as dependent for its display on the human weakness of a traditional Jesus and the womanly tenderness of a traditional Mary. This conception of God has produced the coarse conventional hell of theology, which again has led to the creation of purgatory and masses for the dead, to alleviate the horrors of the system. In asserting the doctrine of justification by faith, the Reformation in great measure restored the lost truth of grace. Mariolatry and purgatory disappeared with the darkness which produced them, but the mediaeval hell remained. Protestantism, however, when separated from spiritual life, is a mere soulless body; and while the religious movement of the present century has deepened faith in the doctrines of the Reformation, those who have resisted its influences are either turning back to Rome or lapsing to infidelity. On the one side, we see a revival of the old errors of intercession for the dead and the power of "*aeonian* fire" to purify the soul. On the other side, the great truths of Christianity are dismissed as narrow cant; the mystery of Divine love to a lost world is degraded to the level of good-natured benevolence to erring creatures; sin is but human frailty, righteousness a myth, and judgment but the appointed means by which the lost of earth shall be fitted for the heaven to which their relationship to God entitles them. In a shallow, and, therefore, a sceptical age, this is the most popular religion. It vaunts itself as the outcome of increased enlightenment; in fact it is but the mingled ignorance and insolence of unbelief.

---

1. Rom. i. 16-18.
2. Heb. vi. 6.
3. The Gospel and its Ministry (4th Ed.),
4. I John iv. 9.
5. John iii. 16.
6. John iii. 18.
7. Gal. vi. 7.
8. Butler, *The Analogy* pt. v., ch. II., § 2.

CHAPTER 13
APPENDIX.

The following are the passages of the New Testament principally relied on to prove the doctrines of universalism. The exposition here offered is commended to the consideration of the reader.

Acts iii. 21

"Whom the heaven must receive until the times of restitution of all things, which God hath spoken by the mouth of all His holy prophets since the world began."—The word here rendered "restitution" occurs nowhere else in the New Testament, but the kindred verb is used in eight passages,[1] two of which throw light on this one. The prophetic Scriptures abound in predictions of a coming period of mingled blessing and judgment upon earth, and the Old Testament closes with the statement that its advent will be heralded by the return of Elijah.[2] This was used by the Scribes to disprove the claims of Jesus to Messiahship, and in Matt. xvii. 1o the disciples referred the difficulty to their Master. The Lord in reply expressly confirmed the prophecy, declaring that "Elias truly shall come first and *restore all things.*"[3]

So again in Mark ix. 12, "Elias verily cometh first and *restoreth all things.*" St. Peter's words, in Acts iii. 21, unmistakably refer to this the common hope of the people he was addressing,—a hope confirmed by Christ Himself. If, even then, Israel would but repent, God would send them the Messiah appointed for them, even Jesus;[4] whom the heaven must receive until the times of *restoration of all things*, of which (times) God spake by the mouth of all His holy prophets since the world began. He goes on to assert emphatically that *every* prophet, from Samuel onwards, foretold of those days, and he ends by connecting with these same prophecies the promise to Abraham that in his Seed all the kindreds of the earth shall be blessed. It is as clear as light, therefore, that "the times of restoration of all things" are no other than "the times of refreshing" of the 19th verse, "the great season of joy and rest *on earth*, which it was understood the coming of Messiah in His glory was to bring with it."[5]

Moreover, "*all* the prophets" "have foretold of

these days," and their voice is almost, if not entirely, silent, about events beyond the last great judgment of "the quick amid dead." We are forced to the conclusion, therefore, that the use which has been made of the apostle's words is a perversion of the Scripture. It must not be overlooked that "the times of restoration of all things" will be marked by the destruction of the obdurate and disobedient.[6]

I Corinthians xv. 22.

"For as in Adam all die, even so in Christ shall all be made alive"—Does this teach universal blessing? The words can be read in two ways. Either "death" may be taken to mean no more than physical death, and "life" as implying only the resurrection; or else the words may be understood in their deeper spiritual significance. If we adopt the former reading, then the passage means that as death is the lot of every human being, so every human being shall be raised from the dead by Christ's power. But who disputes this? It is the common faith of Christendom![7]

But, it will be urged, the words mean more than this: "life" means salvation in the highest sense. Then "death" must be construed on the same principle, for the words are correlatives. How then shall we read the verse? As every human being dies, i.e. shall be finally lost, so every human being shall live, *i.e.* shall be finally saved. But these propositions are contradictory and absurd. We must either be content, therefore, to take the words as asserting merely the universality of death and resurrection, or else we must adopt a second possible rendering,[8] and construe them thus: As in Adam all who belong to Adam die, so in Christ all who belong to Christ shall be made alive. That this is in fact the apostle's meaning the immediate sequel proves. He adds, "But each in his own order; Christ, the firstfruits, afterwards they that are Christ's (*i.e.* who belong to Christ) at His coming." That there will be beyond that "resurrection to life" a resurrection to judgment, we know from other Scriptures; but this is outside the scope of the apostle's argument, and he makes no mention of it here. If the 22nd verse be bracketed with the 21st, it will be read on the first principle above suggested; if with the 23rd, it will be pregnant with higher truth. But in neither case can it have the slightest bearing on the present controversy.

In the passage under consideration the climax is reached in the statement of the 28th verse that the great end of the "mediatorial kingdom" is "that God may be all in all." These words are held to imply universal restoration. But this result is declared to be "when He shall have *put down* all rule, and all authority, and power." It is not attained "till He hath put all enemies under *His feet*" till "all things shall be *subdued* unto Him"; and this is not the sort of language in which Scripture speaks of winning back the lost to God. Moreover, the absolute and acknowleged supremacy of the Almighty is all that is involved in the words "that God may be all in all."

The gloss "all things *in all men*" betrays either dishonesty or levity in handling Scripture. The supremacy is universal, and if it be brought about by reconciliation, the blessing must be shared by all the hosts of darkness.

Philippians ii. 10.

This last remark applies with equal force to the statement of the Divine purpose "that at the name of Jesus every knee should bow, of things in heaven, and things on earth, and things under the earth." Not merely angels and saints and men on earth shall own Him Lord, but also the dwellers in the underworld. But till it has been proved that this acknowledgment shall be obtained from all by reconciliation, it must not be assumed that it will not be, in the case of some, by judgment.

Revelation v. 13; xxi. 4, 5; xxii. 3.

With this statement in Philippians the vision of Rev. v. 13 appears to be connected. But this perhaps has been assumed too easily. The language seems to be figurative, for it is not intelligent beings only, but all animated creation, that join in the anthem of praise. No argument can fairly be based on it.

The use made in this controversy of the description of the blessedness of the redeemed in the new creation must excite surprise in the mind of any one who studies the context. For the redeemed there is to be no more curse or death or sorrow, "but" (in awful contrast with this) "the fearful and unbelieving. . . shall have *their* part in the lake which burneth with fire and brimstone."

Romans v.

It is idle to ignore the fact that theologians widely differ in their exegesis of the 5th chapter of Romans. But all that is essential here is to determine whether the meaning put upon the passage by the advocates of universalism be the true interpretation of it. The difficulty of the passage is centred in the statement of the 18th verse, that "as through one trespass [the judgment came] unto all men to condemnation; even so through one act of righteousness [the free gift came] unto all men to justification of life."[9]

Verses 13 to 17 are parenthetical, and in the apostle's argument the words just quoted follow upon the statement of the 12th verse, that, by reason of Adam's sin, "death passed upon all men." Therefore, he concludes, as the result of that one trespass was unto all men to condemnation, even so the result of Christ's one act of righteousness[10] was unto all men to justification. But surely the second of these correlative clauses is governed by the first. Men have "many trespasses," as the 16th verse declares, and the χάρισμα is "unto justification" from them all. But here he is speaking only of the "*one* trespass," and establishing that the death of Christ has cancelled the effects of Adam's sin.

No one will deny that this is a fair and natural rendering of the passage; and this being so, I might pass on, leaving it to those who insist upon giving it a wider meaning to prove the correctness of their view. But let us pursue the matter further. As the condemnation included "*all* men," so also does the justification which tends to life. That the *saved* will be freed from the guilt of original sin is a mere truism. The apostle's statement is that the benefit is for *all*. Christ has won for mankind immunity from judgment for Adam's sin. So far as regards that sin every human being is "justified."[11]

But we are told we must not thus limit it. What then is the alternative? That just as that "one trespass" brought condemnation upon every human being, even so the death of Christ brought him justification, not from Adam's sin only, but from *all* sin. There is no question here of the penitent believer's blessing, but of the condition of man as man in virtue of the death of Christ. "All men," penitent and impenitent alike, are "justified from all things." All sins are thus wiped out for ever; and yet these same teachers tell us that for these very sins the sinner shall be punished "in aeonian fire beyond the grave"!

Ephesians i. 10.

The Epistle to the Ephesians announces the purpose of God "that in the dispensation of the fulness of times He might gather together in one all things in Christ, the things in the heavens and the things on the earth." The words "all things" (τὰ πάντα) shall be further considered under the next passage cited. Suffice it here to admit that they are wide enough to include the universe, and if explanatory words of as wide signification be added, no other meaning can fairly be put on them. But is it clear that the words here added are not words of *limitation*? In the passage already noticed in Philippians, where the supremacy of Christ is in question, the apostle includes, with heaven and earth, the *underworld*; and that "the heavens" include the abode of fallen angels and lost men is a startling assumption which cannot be conceded. Moreover, it is admitted by all that the lost will be sent to their punishment *after* the last great judgment. Therefore if they are to be included in the "gathering together," "the economy of the fulness of times" must be explained on a principle unknown to theologians. Further, the rendering "gather together in one" gives to the word here used a colour which scarcely belongs to it. It occurs once again—viz., in Rom. xiii. 9., where the apostle says the law is *briefly comprehended* in the one word which enjoins love. The word means to *head up* or *sum up,* as *ex. gr.* at the close of a speech. The universe shall yet be headed up in Christ. He shall regain the place from which sin has sought to dethrone Him. But whether this shall be accomplished by the restoration of all, or by the subjection of all, we must turn to other scriptures to decide.

Colossians i. 20.

The most important passage still remains. To the Colossians St. Paul writes thus: "For in Him" (Christ) "God was pleased that the whole fulness should dwell, and by Him to reconcile again all things to Him, having made peace by means of the blood of His cross—through Him—whether the things on the earth or the .things in the heavens." (I have followed the translation given in Alford's Commentary.) Here at last we have a statement which, it ought to be admitted, *seems* to teach universal restoration. To attempt a critical analysis of the somewhat conflicting views of commentators on the passage would involve too serious a digression. But in accordance with the scheme of my argument, the following suggestions are offered for the consideration of the thoughtful.

First, then, the remark already made on the words "all things" applies here with increased force. It cannot be questioned that in the 16th verse these words have no limitation whatever; for in speaking of *creation*, "the heavens and the earth" include the universe in every part and to its utmost limits. But sin has produced an apostasy from "the heavens and the earth," and as already noticed, the apostle when asserting Christ's supremacy enumerates the heavens, the earth, and the *underworld*. Further; there is sometimes a good deal of theology in the use of the Greek article, and its presence here indicates that the prominent thought in the passage is not every part of the universe, but the universe regarded as a whole. May not the lapsed portion of it be ignored here, as it is ignored in the closing words of the first chapter of the Bible, where *everything*[12] that God had made was declared to be very good, albeit the Serpent and his angels had already marred the unity of creation?

But it is the word "reconcile" upon which attention must be centred in considering this passage. It is used only by St. Paul, and the passages in which it occurs are so few and so important that it will be well to quote them here.

Rom. v. 10.–"For if when we were enemies, we *were reconciled* to God by the death of His Son, much more, *being reconciled*, we shall be saved by His life."

Rom. v. ii.—"Christ, by whom we have now received the *atonement*."

Rom. xi. 15.— "If the casting away of them" (Israel) "be the *reconciling* of the world."

I Cor. vii. 11.— "Let her . . *be reconciled* to her husband."

II Cor. v. 18-20.—"All things are of God, Who hath reconciled us to Himself by Jesus Christ, and hath given to us the ministry of *reconciliation*, to wit, that God was in Christ *reconciling*[13] the world unto Himself, . . . and hath committed unto us the word of *reconciliation*[14] . . We pray in Christ's stead be ye *reconciled* to God."

Eph. ii. 16.—"That He *might reconcile* both" (Jew and Gentile) "unto God in one body by the cross."

Col. i. 20, 21.—"Having made peace through the blood of His cross, by Him *to reconcile*[15] all things unto Himself: by Him, whether they be things on earth or things in heaven. And you that were sometimes alienated and enemies in your mind by wicked works, yet now *hath* He *reconciled* in the body of His flesh through death."

This word translated "reconcile" means, first,

to change one thing for another; and, secondly, as here, to change a person from enmity to friendship. The question at once suggests itself, On which side is the change? Is it in God's attitude towards the creature, or in the creature's attitude towards God? Does the creature receive God into his favour, or is it God Who receives the creature? The mere statement of the question seems to prejudge the answer. In a case like this there is no safer clue to the meaning of any word in the New Testament than its use in the Septuagint. Dean Alford quotes the following as the places where it occurs:—

Jer. xxxi. (xlviii.) 39 (a mistranslation).

II Macc. i. 5, "God . . . hear your prayers and *be reconciled* unto you;" vii. 33, "Though the living Lord be angry with us . . . yet shall He *be reconciled* unto His servants"; viii. 29, "They besought the merciful Lord to *be reconciled* unto His servants for ever."

As regards the noun (καταλλαγή), Archbishop Trench[16] says it only occurs twice in the Septuagint, and in one of these passages it means simply exchange. In the other passage, II Macc. v. 20, "it is employed in the New Testament sense." There the writer says, speaking of the Temple, "As it was forsaken in the wrath of the Almighty, so again, on the reconciliation of time great Lord, it was set up with all glory." Dr. Trench goes on to say that the Christian reconciliation is, *first*, "a reconciliation effected once for all for us by Christ upon His cross;" though it is, "secondly and subordinately," "the daily deposition under the operation of the Holy Spirit of the enmity of the old man toward God." And the writer adds, "All attempt to make this, the secondary meaning of the word, to be the primary, rests not on an unprejudiced exegesis, but on a foregone determination to get rid of the reality of God's anger against sin." These are weighty words, of special moment here.

In all these passages from the Septuagint reconciliation is from God to man; and if with the light they give we turn back to the scriptures above set forth, this same conclusion will be established. "We *were reconciled* to God by the death of His Son." On conversion the sinner did not produce, he only *"received* the reconciliation." Is it not clear as light that it is this accomplished reconciliation which has dethroned sin and ushered in the reign of grace?

The next passage is still more unmistakable. The setting aside of Israel was "the reconciliation of the world."[17] When Israel rejected Messiah, God set the nation aside and turned toward the world. Again, "God was in Christ reconciling the world to Himself." "It is not a present work, but a work past and finished. By that death we who were enemies were reconciled. The appeal of the Gospel is now that men would receive the reconciliation. 'Be reconciled to God' is not an entreaty to time sinner to forgive his God, but an appeal to him to come within the reconciliation God has wrought."[18]

All this leads unmistakably to the conclusion that "the reconciliation of all things" is not a hope to be fulfilled in the coming eternity, but a fact accomplished in the death of Christ. It is impossible that the way of life ever can become more free than that death has made it; and if men refuse the proffered mercy, if they reject the reconciliation, what alternative can there be but wrath?

John i. 29.

"Behold the Lamb of God, which taketh away the sin of the world."— The only question we have to consider here is whether the record of this utterance of the Baptist is to be taken as a doctrinal statement proving universal expiation. It is unnecessary, therefore, to discuss the views of rival commentators upon the text, especially as, apart from controversy, no one probably would question its reference to Isaiah liii. 6, 7, which again contains an allusion to the "scapegoat" of Lev. xvi. 21, It is as though the Baptist had exclaimed, "Behold Him Who is the fulfilment of the 53rd chapter of Isaiah." It was a testimony to the Messiahship of Jesus; and it is unwarrantable to read it as though it were designed to settle in advance the controversy between the Calvinist and the Universalist. The one, no doubt, is bound to reconcile the words with his narrow views of redemption, and the other must account for the fact of judgment to come, consistently with universal expiation. But they who refuse to take either side in that controversy will be content to mark that while the work of Christ has a relation to the world, it has not brought the world deliverance from judgment. The question here involved is not the duration of future punishment, but whether future punishment is possible at all.[19]

1 Timothy ii. 4,6; iv. 10.

God "will have all men to be saved." Christ "gave Himself a ransom for all." God "is the Saviour of all men, specially of those that believe."

The exposition of previous passages renders it almost unnecessary to say anything about these. Judgment and hell are facts which all admit. Whatever these verses mean, therefore, they are consistent with the perdition of the ungodly. If Christ were not a ransom for *all*, there would be those on earth whom God could not save. Grace, therefore, would be in chains, and not enthroned. This word *ransom* occurs here only. The kindred word is used in Matt. xx. 28 and Mark x. 45.

The 4th verse, as it reads in the English, may mean either that God intends to save all men, or else that He is willing that all should be saved. There is no such ambiguity in the Greek, The statement is akin to that of 2 Peter iii. 9, "The Lord is... not willing that any should perish, but that all should come to repentance." God has revealed Himself as "the Saviour of all men"? But if He be *in the same sense* the Saviour of all, what possible meaning can there be in the words of limitation, "specially of those that believe." As it has been well put, As far as salvation stands in Him, He is the Saviour of all men; but it is only in those who believe that the salvation becomes actual.

Matthew v. 26

"Thou shalt by no means come out thence till thou hast paid the uttermost farthing."—As Dean Alford remarks, "These words, which in the earthly example imply future liberation, because an earthly debt can be paid in most cases, so in the spiritual counterpart amount to a negation of it, because the debt can never be discharged." Indeed, the use of this text in support of universalism only betokens the weakness of the cause; for imprisonment for debt is the basis of the parable, and this necessarily implies discharge when the debt is paid. The only possible way in which the idea of discharge on payment could be negatived would be by fixing the debt at a sum entirely beyond the power of any man to pay. And this is precisely what the Lord has done in the kindred passage, Matt. xviii. 24. There, again, the debtor was committed "till he should pay all that was due"; but the sum due was so enormous that payment was impossible. If the 10,000 talents were of *gold*, the amount was fabulous. But even if of silver, the mention of such an amount would have impressed, and was clearly intended to impress, the hearers with the idea of hopeless ruin. It was the sum at which Haman reckoned the revenue derivable from the destruction of the entire Jewish people (Esther ii. 9).

John iii. 17, xii. 32.

"God sent not His Son into the world to condemn the world, but that the world through Him might be saved."—This may express either the desire that all may be saved, or the intention that all shall be saved. Does the context leave it doubtful which is meant? The preceding verse expressly limits the actual blessing to the believer; and the verse which follows declares in the plainest terms not merely that the rejecter of Christ shall be condemned—which is the antithesis of being saved,—but that "he is *condemned already*." And the chapter closes with the words, "He that believeth not the Son *shall not see life*, but the wrath of God abideth on him." The use made of the passage, therefore, to prove universalism can only avail to suggest the sad inquiry whether any honesty is to be looked for in religious controversy.[20]

The last passage which claims attention is the record of words spoken by the Blessed Lord shortly before His crucifixion, "And I, if I be lifted up from the earth, will draw all unto Me." "This He said" (the universalist declares) "signifying that all men are ultimately to be saved." "This He said" (the inspired evangelist adds) *signifying what death He should die.*" The statement, in fact, has no bearing on the controversy. In the days of His humiliation the Lord declared that no one could come to Him unless drawn by the Father Who had sent Him: in view of His cross He announced the time was coming when He would draw all to Himself. But the question before us now is the future of those who resist the influence; and on this the testimony of Scripture is given in no doubtful terms.

CONCLUSION

The list of texts given by the author first quoted in these pages is swelled by several from the Old Testament. Most of these fall within the general remarks made *supra*, the exceptions being passages which the reader will study in vain to discover how they bear upon the question at all.[21] Indeed, this writer's appeal to Scripture is an enigma, considering that he distinctly repudiates belief in universalism.

There are many other passages, of course, freely used by universalists, which have not been noticed here. Romans xi. 26 is an example. "All Israel shall be saved." This means either that every Israelite, from Patriarchal times to the end of the world, will ultimately be saved or else that in days to come Israel *as a nation* shall be saved. Can any one doubt which is the true interpretation? In the context it is expressly stated that in the Divine intention Israel does not embrace every Israelite (ix. 6); and this same apostle's testimony to the Jews included a warning that perdition was the doom of despisers (Acts xiii. 41).

As a typical instance of passages which are not quoted by writers of this school may be cited Luke xiii. 23-8. "Said one unto Him, Lord, are there few that be saved? And He said unto them, Strive to enter in at the strait gate; for many, I say unto you, will seek to enter in and *shall not be able*." When will that be? He goes on to explain that the day is coming when the door which now stands open shall be closed, and then the sinner will knock at it in vain. At the very epoch when, these teachers tell us, the door will be flung open for *all*, the Lord Himself declares it will be closed even against those who seek an entrance.

---

1. Matt. xii. 13, xvii. 11; Mark iii. 5, viii. 25, ix. 12; Luke vi. 10; Acts i. 6; Heb. xiii. 19.
2. Mal. iv. 5.
3. "Our Lord speaks here plainly in the future, and uses the very word of the prophecy (Mal. iv. 6). The *double* allusion

is only the assertion that the Elias (in spirit and power) who foreran our Lord's first coming was a partial fulfilment of the great prophecy which announces the real Elias"— Alford, on Matt. xvii. 11.
4. The Authorised Version fails to give the meaning of the original.
5. Alford, *in loco*.
6. Compare ver. 23 with what goes before.
7. I pass by special questions which might be raised as to whether death be *in fact* the lot of all. It certainly is not, as ver. 51 expressly states.
8. The passage might, no doubt, be read that just as the sin of Adam, if left to work out its results unhindered, would lead to the perdition of all men, so, on the same principle, the death of Christ would lead to their salvation. But this would not advance the argument the least, and it is not pretended that it is the meaning of the passage.
9. The words in square brackets are not expressed in the original.
10. "The death of Christ viewed as the acme of His obedience." See Alford on Phil. ii. 8.
11. If any should shrink from the use of the word "justification" in respect of any but the saved, will they consider what other word would convey the truth involved? Forgiveness would be a faulty substitute, and clearly inaccurate, and with God immunity from punishment assumes the absence of guilt.
12. τὰ πάντα: Gen. i. 31 (lxx).
13. καταλλάσσω.
14. καταλλαγή.
15. ἀποκαταλλάττω.
16. Synonyms (second series).
17. The A.V., in translating the word by a verb, suggests a gradual reconciling; but this is misleading.
18. *The Gospel and its Ministry*, p. 131.
19. Having learned to trust the absolute accuracy of Scripture, I have no doubt there is a designed distinction between "the *sin* of the world" and "the *sins* of the world." But as I do not pretend to write a commentary on these passages, the above exposition is carried no further than

the subject requires. Let it not be forgotten that they who deny the verbal inspiration of Scripture arc merely quibbling when they rely on any such statement as the Baptist's to prove anything.
20. The above remarks apply also to John xii. 47, "I came not to judge the world, but to save the world."
21. The following is the list:— Gen. iii. 15, xii. 3; Psalm ciii. 9, cxxxix. 8; Lam. iii. 31-3; Isa. lvii. 16, xlv. 21, xlix. 9, liii. 11; Hos, vi. i, xiv. 4; Micah vii. 18, 19.

Copyright © 2023 by Alicia EDITIONS

Credits: Alicia EDITIONS, www.canva.com

PAPERBACK: 9782384551941

E-BOOK: 9782384551958

HARDCOVER: 9782384551965

All rights reserved.

No part of this book may be reproduced in any form or by any electronic or mechanical means, including information storage and retrieval systems, without written permission from the author, except for the use of brief quotations in a book review.

www.ingramcontent.com/pod-product-compliance
Lightning Source LLC
LaVergne TN
LVHW032012070526
838202LV00059B/6411